The Grimoire of Tiamat

THE GRIMOIRE OF TIAMAT

Asenath Mason

The Grimoire of Tiamat

ISBN: 978-0-9830639-6-4

Published by Nephilim Press
A division of Nephilim Press LLC
www.nephilimpress.com

Contents

BOOK 3
APPENDICES

INTRODUCTION

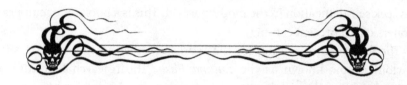

In the Aeon of Re-Awakening, forgotten gods and spirits rise to reveal their teachings to those who do not fear to embrace the Gnosis that was shunned and abhorred for centuries and labeled as "demonic," "devilish" or "forbidden." The bad reputation of the Left Hand Path rests on its antinomian and transgressive practices, which are tempting and attractive in their promise of transforming Man into God. These practices are also viewed as fearful and dangerous, however, as they shatter and rebuild every single aspect of individual psyche, personal life and the whole perception of the surrounding world. Not everyone is ready for this change, and for many potential initiates, the Path becomes a horrible trauma instead of a beautiful and liberating spiritual adventure. The teachings revealed in this book are not for everyone either. Casual experimentation with this Work is strongly discouraged, as these rituals open the gateways of the soul that can never be closed again. The Gnosis of Tiamat, the Primal Dragon Goddess, is terrifying, demanding and transformative on all possible levels of existence. It will take the practitioner to the very Womb of Chaos where the soul will be devoured, dissolved, transformed and reborn, in order to become the Dragon in essence, the living incarnation of this primordial Current.

Even though Tiamat and the myth of Creation, which inspired the Work of this grimoire, are derived from the ancient Babylonian lore, the ritual system presented here can hardly be called "Babylonian magic," and it does not claim to be such. There are no archeological findings or historical accounts that would confirm any form of worship of the primal gods or demonic beings created by the Dragon Goddess. The only mentions of demons and evil spirits are found in exorcisms and banishing formulas. Therefore, rituals presented in this book do not revive any ancient traditions and are not re-construction of any lost magical systems. Instead, they constitute a frame-work for the application of Gnosis that was revealed through the teachings of the demon-gods themselves and are laid down here specifically for those who seek self-deification in the modern world. This is a book for occult prac-titioners of the present century.

The foremost inspiration for the Work described in this book was the Babylonian epic known as the *Enuma Elish*. The research literature on the myth of Creation is almost solely focused on Marduk and his role in Babylonian magic and religion, while Tiamat and her Children are hardly mentioned at all. The only available information is the analysis of the elev-en demon-gods from the linguistic perspective and their occasional meta-phorical interpretations, such as their connection to astrology, which is the domain which made the Babylonians famous across the ancient world. The original magical meaning, however, seems to be lost. In this book, there are no rituals and workings devoted to Marduk. I leave this field to his follow-ers and devotees. This is the book of Tiamat and the primal demon-gods who were born in her Black Waters of Chaos. Here, we will look at each de-mon-god from their historical and linguistic meaning, as well, but the main purpose of this grimoire is to present the Children of Tiamat from their esoteric perspective and to explore their magical powers as they manifest to the modern practitioner. The linguistic and astrological interpretation quot-ed in this grimoire is based on such works as Stephen Langdon's *Babylonian Epic of Creation*, F.A.M. Wiggerman's *Mesopotamian Protective Spirits* and Leonard King's *Enuma Elish, The Seven Tablets of Creation*. For other sourc-es, it is recommended to view the bibliography listed by the end of this book.

The occult interpretation and the practical part of this grimoire is based on materials gathered during my personal work with Tiamat and her de-mon-gods in the years 2007-2012. The Work started as a magical project conducted by Lodge Magan, the occult ritual group that was founded in the beginning of the last decade in order to earth and channel the Dra-conian Current through practical application of the Left-Hand-Path phi-losophy. The purpose of the project, which started by the end of 2007, was to gather information about the nature of the eleven spirits, their magical powers and methods of how they can be used for self-initiatory work in the magic of the twenty-first century. The project was also conducted in several phases, according to a carefully chosen curriculum, which included a wide spectrum of practices, from simple visual meditations, scrying and dream travels to more advanced works of invocation, evocation, journeys through hidden gateways and dimensions and exploration of forgotten worlds and lost temples.

The teachings presented on the pages of this grimoire are derived from my personal experience, but they were also tested by ritual friends, partners and those who sought knowledge and power in the Gnosis of the Primal Dragon Goddess. Those reluctant to work with "unverified gnosis" will not find it here. All rituals described in this book were performed and their results were verified to prove their efficacy, both through self-initiatory work and through manifestation of their results on the physical plane. Therefore, they provide a solid ritual system which lays foundations for the further work with this forgotten Gnosis. It is my personal hope and wish that this book will find its way into the hands of those who will not hesitate to embark on the journey to the Womb of Darkness, reach for the primal wisdom and power and carry the Dragon's Fire as a torch to illuminate the Path for others.

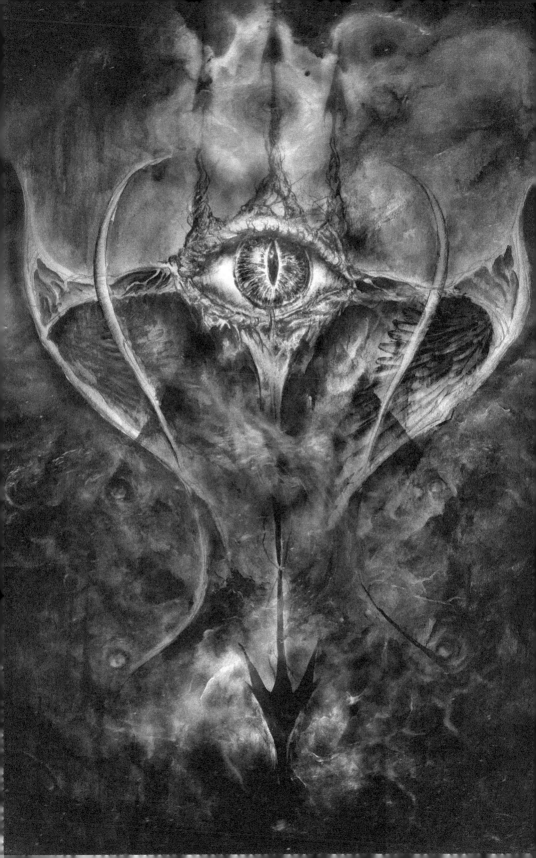

BOOK 1

PRIMAL
DRACONIAN GODS

Tiamat,
Her Origin and Mythology

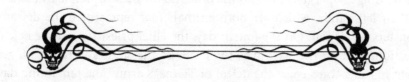

Enuma Elish

he story of Tiamat and her eleven monsters derives from the Babylonian Creation epic, the *Enuma Elish*, named after its opening words, "When in the height." Also known as *The Seven Tablets of Creation*, this epic is one of the central works in Babylonian mythology and one of the oldest Creation legends in the world. The myth exists in several versions from Babylonia and Assyria, the most known being the one found in Nineveh, in the library of King Ashurbanipal, which dates to the 7th century BCE. The legend itself, however, is far older and it is estimated to be dated as far back as the 18th century BCE, the time of a prominent status of the god, Marduk, the leading deity of the Babylonian pantheon, who also occupies the central position in the story.

The *Enuma Elish* was first recovered by Henry Layard in 1849 in Nineveh and published by George Smith in 1870s as *The Chaldaean Account of Genesis*. It consists of about 1000 lines on seven clay tablets. The fifth tablet is particularly damaged and its content has never been recovered in full. The most important, however, is the text of the fourth tablet, which was published in 1887 by E.A. Wallis Budge and translated by A. Sayce. The central theme of the myth is the elevation of Marduk above all other Babylonian gods and his creation of the world and mankind from the primordial Darkness and Chaos, which he closed within the frames of a structured order. Therefore, the whole story presented in the *Enuma Elish* is, in fact, a praise of Marduk, the creator of heaven and earth, and the lord of the world.

From the account of Akkadian rituals described in *Rituels Accadiens* by F. Thureau-Dangin (1921), we learn that the epic was recited in Babylon during celebrations of the New Year. On the second day of the festival, a priest of Marduk recited a hymn about the victory of the god over Tiamat and her allies. On the third day, artists made two statues for the celebrations: one holding a viper (*bašmu*) and the other holding a scorpion (*akrabamêlu*) in their left hands, which are both animals that represented the defeated monsters of Tiamat. On the fourth day, the chief priest recited the epic of Creation. And on the sixth day, the heads of the statues were cut off and burnt in order to re-enact the defeat of Tiamat's army. The remaining days were devoted to the praise of the gods and on the eleventh day, the gods returned to their temples and the celebrations were over. The epic had a similar status in Assyria, though with one major difference – Marduk was here replaced by Ašur, the chief Assyrian deity.

According to the legend, in the beginning, there was nothing but the world of primordial waters swirling in Chaos, undifferentiated and infinite. Then, the waters divided into sweet, fresh waters of Apsū and salty waters of Tiamat, the two primeval gods, traditionally depicted as the male and the female, the first divine couple, and the parents to all gods and all life. Apart from them, there was also a mysterious entity named Mummu, which took the form of the mist floating above the waters and was sometimes referred to as "the vizier" of Apsū. The union of the primordial couple gave birth to the other deities: Lahmu and Lahamu, who, in turn, were parents of Anshar and Kishar (identified with the heaven and the earth). These two had a son, Anu, who fathered Nudimmud, the greatest of the gods (god Ea). The younger gods were very loud and disturbed the sleep of Apsū, distracting him from his rest. Upon the advice of Mummu, his vizier, he decided to kill them, but Tiamat strongly opposed the plan. In order to prevent the murder, she warned Nudimmud, who put a spell on Apsū and killed him, creating his abode on the remains of his slain father. Now, Nudimmud became the chief god and with his consort, Damkina, he had a son, Marduk, who was even more powerful than himself. When Marduk was playing with winds, creating storms and tornadoes, he disturbed the sleep of the old gods again. Enraged by the noise, they persuaded Tiamat that she should seek revenge for the death of her husband. Upon their advice, she took another consort, the god Kingu, and gave him command over her new army – the eleven terrible monsters whom she had created to fight in the war. These eleven monsters represent her eleven dark powers which oppose the powers of the Light. Tiamat also bestowed on Kingu the Tablet of Destinies, a mythical emblem of the supreme authority over the universe. Until that moment, this dominion had belonged to the Mother Goddess alone, the supreme mistress of the universe and all Creation. The younger gods chose Marduk as their champion and commander of their army, and endowed him with the power of the four winds. In the battle which took place between the worlds, Marduk defeated Tiamat and split her flesh into two halves. From one of them, he fashioned the earth and from the other, the sky. Her weeping eyes became the source of the rivers and her breasts formed the mountains of the earth. He took the Tablet of Destinies from Kingu, and he forced the gods who sided with Tiamat to work in service for the other gods. Eventually, he killed Kingu and from his blood, Nudimmud (Ea) created mankind whose task was to replace the gods in their work. Babylon was established as the residence of the chief gods and Marduk was elevated by receiving fifty names in praise of his great powers.

THE FIRST MOTHER

In the *Enuma Elish,* Tiamat is described as "Ummu-Hubur who formed all things." The name "Hubur" sometimes refers to the river in the underworld. She is also related to the Hebrew concept of *Tehom,* the great deep of the primordial waters. Tiamat and Apsū personify the cosmic abyss filled with primal energies which preceded the original Creation, while Apsū's vizier, Mummu, is thought to be the archetypal watery form, and his name is sometimes translated as "mold, matrix."[1] The ancient Mesopotamians believed that the world was a flat circular disc surrounded by a saltwater sea. The earth was a continent which floated on a second sea, the freshwater *apsu* from which all waters, including springs, rivers, wells and lakes, flowed on the land. The sky was a solid disc above the earth, which curved to touch the earth at its rim. The heaven, or the habitation of the gods, was above the sky.

The first Mother Goddess was the primordial source of all life, the embodiment of Primal Chaos, the Cosmic Womb which gave birth to all gods and all souls. She held dominion over the forces of Creation and she possessed the power to shape destinies, which is symbolic of the supreme

---

[1] Thorkild Jacobsen: *The Treasures of Darkness.* A History of Mesopotamian Religion

authority over the whole universe. In the *Enuma Elish*, "when of the gods none had been called into being, and none bore a name, and no destinies were ordained," she was the first force of Creation, the origin of life, the source of all movement and evolution. However, when she turned against her own children, the younger generation of gods, she also became the force of destruction, the devouring monster, the ever-gaping womb and the mother of abominations. Once a caring and nurturing parent, she turned into a vengeful warrior goddess, the mother of monsters and all evil of the world.

As the goddess of primordial waters, Tiamat was often portrayed in a monstrous, bestial form and imagined as a sea serpent or a dragon. However, not much is known about her appearance from the myth itself. In this sense, she is identified with the sea monsters from other mythologies, such as the biblical Leviathan, Yamm and Lotan from the Hebrew myths or Tannin, the sea demon from the Jewish legends. Etymologically, her name corresponds to such terms as the Greek word *thalassa*, "sea," Semitic *tehom*, "abyss," Akkadian *ti'amtum* and *tâmtu*, "sea," or Sumerian *ti* and *ama*, meaning "life" and "mother." Francois Lenormant, in his *Chaldean Magic Its Origin and Development*, mentions also such names as Tauthe of Damascius and Thavath-Omoroca, the latter being a form of the Great Mother as a type of the watery abyss, possibly inspired by the account of the Creation given by Berossus in his *History of Babylonia*. There are also many theories concerning the possible meaning of the myth, in which the primordial state of "mixing of the waters" is interpreted as the meeting of salty and fresh waters in the Persian Gulf; the creation of gods and monsters is thought to refer to the rise of volcanoes and tectonic movements; or the battle of Tiamat and Marduk is viewed as a cosmic catastrophe in which the presently existing planets were created. Since no unanimous interpretation exists, the myth still leaves a great field for possible speculations.

Tiamat, above all, is the universal Mother who gives birth to all creation in her womb, the salty waters. This was the original habitation of the gods before Marduk created the earth and chose Babylon as his residence, while the gods moved to live in the heaven. Marduk does not possess the natural power of creation – his power is the divine speech, the attribute of all patriarchal gods from world's religions. In the *Enuma Elish,* he has to prove that he possesses this power before he is allowed to face Tiamat in the battle. He is given a garment which he has to destroy and restore by the power of his word before he is entrusted by the gods as their champion.

As the Mother of Creation, Tiamat is sometimes identified with the Sumerian goddess, Nammu, the mistress of the primordial sea who gave birth to An and Ki, the heaven and the earth. They both were thought to personify the constellation in the northern sky known today as "the whale." In ancient times, it was called by the names of sea monsters, Tiamat or Cetus. It is located in the region of the sky known as the Water, along with other watery constellations, such as Aquarius, Pisces or Eridanus. In the myth of Enki and the creation of man, Nammu (also called Ninmah) is described as "the primeval sea," "the mother who gave birth to all the gods." Enki seeks her assistance in his work of creation, as he himself has no power to fashion a human being:

> "O my mother, the creature whose name you uttered, it exists,
> Bind upon it the image of the gods;
> Mix the heart of the clay that is over the abyss...
> You, do bring the limbs into existence...;
> O my mother, decree its fate."[2]

The creature fashioned by Enki is feeble and weak, for only the Mother Goddess has the power to create life and breathe the soul into the vessel of clay.

But the salty waters of seas and oceans can hardly be considered a nourishing substance. They do not quench the thirst of living beings and they do not make the crops grow. The waters of Tiamat are dissolving, corroding, poisonous and deadly. Opposed to them are the fresh waters of Apsū, the source of all lakes, rivers, springs and wells, the life-giving waters of the earth. *Apsu, abzu,* or *engur* (or *engurru*), originally part of the cosmic Chaos, was transformed into the source of nourishing waters existing under the ground, as subterranean reservoirs and the veins of the earth. The name of this principle, as well as the mythology, depends on the tradition. The Akkadian and Assyrian *abzu* or *apsú* was the subterranean ocean, but it was also the great reservoir of cosmic waters surrounding the earth. In Sumerian legends, *apsu* is the kingdom of Enki (Ea), "the lord of wisdom," but also the abode of sea monsters that are sent after Inanna when she descends to the watery abyss in order to obtain the *me*'s, the divine decrees, which she needs to win the authority over the gods. The watery kingdom is transformed into the house of wisdom after Apsū is slain by his eldest son, but it retains its

---

2   Samuel Noah Kramer: *The Sumerians.* Their History, Culture, and Character

chaotic and destructive quality, still personified by monsters and abominations of the sea. Enki's temple in the city of Eridu was believed to be built on *apzu* and known as "the house of cosmic waters." From there, Enki (Ea) controlled Mummu, "the original watery form," thus creating and shaping the world with the multiplicity of forms, while Apsu himself remained motionless and still, resting in eternal sleep. Mesopotamian temples often had pools or watery basins which represented the concept of *apsu,* the subterranean source of water.

THE DRAGON-SLAYING MYTH

In Mesopotamian tradition, we can find several versions of the legend in which the primordial monster is slain by a god or a hero who represents the new world order. Marduk's defeat of Tiamat is the one that inspired the work of this grimoire, therefore it deserves to be discussed in detail. It is also worth mentioning that Tiamat was not the only dragon slain in the cosmic transition from Chaos to Order. Most of these stories refer to killing a serpent, a dragon or a monster that lives in the bottom of the Great Below, in the realm of primeval waters.

The Sumerian god of stormy south wind, Ninurta, is the main character of another dragon-slaying myth called "The Feats and Exploits of Ninurta." This time, the adversary is Asag, the demon of sickness and disease, whose abode is the nether world, or *Kur*. With the destruction of Asag, the primeval waters of the Kur rise to the surface and cover the land of Sumer. The fresh waters are flooded by poisonous waters of the underworld and all vegetation withers. Famine roams across the land and the great calamity falls upon the fields and the cities. Ninurta has to set up a pile of stones like a great wall to divide Sumer from the Kur and to hold back "the mighty waters." Asag is pictured as a dragon and he seems to be an entity related to Tiamat. Even though these two mythological figures cannot be identified, Asag can be rather viewed as one of Tiamat's Children, monsters born in her Womb, dwelling among the primordial waters of Chaos.

Another Sumerian dragon-slaying myth is the story of the water-god, Enki, defeating "the monster Kur" who abducted the sky-goddess, Ereshkigal, into the underworld. The legend is incomplete and the ending is missing, but from the existing parts, we learn that he attacked Enki's boat with the primeval waters which were his domain. Hence, he seems to be but another monster related to the Dragon Goddess.

The monster Kur is also the adversary in the myth of Inanna's glorification of power. In the story, the goddess of love and battle decides to proclaim her supremacy over the demon and unless he submits to her might and power, she declares to destroy him. And so, she opens the "house of battle" and defeats the monster, after which she gains the epithet "destroyer of Kur," regularly ascribed to her in the hymns.[3]

Finally, there is also the story of the hero Gilgamesh who kills the monster Huwawa, the guardian of the Cedar Forest, or "Land of the Living." Huwawa is not, however, a watery demon and he has no direct connection to the primordial waters of the Void. Nevertheless, the story might have been the original source of the legend of St. George slaying the dragon. Also, his appearance implies that he was born in the Womb of Chaos, like the other monsters and demons spawned by Tiamat. His face is described as composed of coiled entrails of men and beasts, sometimes resembling a lion, and he can kill with his gaze alone. His roar is the flood, his mouth is death and his breath is fire. He is fearsome and terrifying, and he possesses powers that surpass the skills of any human being. Gilgamesh has to trick him to give up these powers before he can eventually defeat him.

The monstrous forms of demons composed of parts borrowed from animals and beasts were symbolic of the primordial character of beings born in the darkness of chaos, in the Primal Womb of the Dragon. Tiamat herself came to be depicted as a hybrid of animal parts, reflecting the disorder of the primordial Darkness, the abyss of non-being. In a bas-relief found in the temple of Ninib at Nimrūd, depicting her fight with Marduk, she has the body, the head and the fore-legs of a lion and the wings, the tail and the hind claws of an eagle. The neck and the upper part of the body are covered with feathers or scales. She represents all that is terrifying, the foul, the abominable, and she is the Mother and the Queen of all fiends, demons and monsters. She is all that lurks behind the Gates of the Night, beyond the safe boundaries of human perception. She manifests through dreams and nightmares, the unknown and the unconscious. The younger generation of gods, however, is usually presented in the human form, in order to represent the comprehensible world, the visible and the familiar.

There is also an interesting description of Tiamat in another myth of Marduk (Bēl) defeating the monster. The Dragon Goddess is huge and measures fifty *kaspu* (*which* was the space that could be covered in two hours

---

[3] Samuel Noah Kramer: *Sumerian Mythology*

travel, i.e. six or seven miles) in length and one *kaspu* in height, with the mouth reaching six cubits (traditional unit of length, based on the length of the forearm) and a tail so long that it reaches the sky. This gives a picture of a giant monster with the body extending for over three hundred miles and raising the head in the air to a height of six or seven miles.[4]

THE PRIMAL CHAOS

The motif of Chaos preceding creation is found in mythologies worldwide. It is usually described as Darkness or Night, the Void, the Gaping Abyss, or Ocean of Black Waters. In the Greek lore this is Tartarus, in Scandinavian myths it is Ginnungagap, Egyptian cosmogony includes the primeval ocean of Nun, and in the Sumerian tradition we have the primordial watery abyss of Apsū and Tiamat. The Womb of Chaos is the birthplace and the abode of dragons, giants, monsters, demons, and primal gods. It is the *tôhû wâ-bhôhû*, the formless void described in *Genesis*. The black waters of the First Mother are like the cosmic ocean of Nun. She is called the Deep, the Void, the Womb, and the Abyss. Gerald Massey associates the waters of Nun with Tepht, the abyss, the source of all life, and equates them with Tiamat, the Great Mother. Tepht is the well from whence the waters issue, the dwelling underground, where the Dragon gave birth to her brood of monsters on the earth. It is the "lair of the dragon," "the hole of the snake."[5] It is also the mythical birthplace of life and vegetation, water to drink, food to eat and air to breathe, the womb of the Cosmic Mother.

As the watery Chaos, Tiamat is identified with the Hebrew concept of *Tehōm,* which means "the deep." There is also a slight resemblance between these two accounts of Creation, as they both include the motif of dividing the waters under the firmament from the waters above. In the Babylonian myth, Marduk splits the body of Tiamat and from her flesh, he fashions the firmament which keeps her upper waters in place, forming the heavenly ocean above the covering of heaven. It is not clear what happens to the lower waters, but a part of them is believed to form Hubur, the river of the underworld. The epic also mentions the so-called *Ti-amat e-li-ti* and *Ti-amat šap-li-ti,* the Upper Tiamat and the Lower Tiamat, which are equivalents of the waters above and under the firmament.[6] And although there are several

---

[4] Leonard W. King: *Enuma Elish*
[5] Gerald Massey: *Ancient Egypt: The Light of the World*
[6] Leonard W. King: *Enuma Elish*

other cosmogonic concepts in the Mesopotamian lore, in all of them, the origin of life and all Creation is the primeval sea which was not created but exists eternally, with no beginning and no end. The primordial waters beget the heaven and the earth, at first united together as the cosmic mountain, then differentiated into the male and the female in order to conceive the younger generations of gods. The Primal Mother is either the sea or the earth, identified with such goddesses as Ninmah, "great queen;" Ninhursag, "queen of the cosmic mountain;" or Nintu, "queen who gives birth." The world is composed of Heaven, consisting of the sky and the space above the sky which is called "the great above," and Earth, consisting of the surface of the earth and "the great below" which is thought to be the underworld and the abode of chthonic deities.[7]

The primal Mother Goddess in the Mesopotamian lore is the "first one, who gave birth to the gods of the universe," "the Mother of Everything," the self-procreating womb, the goddess without a spouse, the primal matter. She is "the womb of abundance," the fertile and fertilizing waters which create spontaneously, All in One, the universe as a whole. She is the Primal Dragon of the Void, the Single Mother, the self-contained Womb. The division of *prima materia* into the masculine and the feminine element is the beginning of the process of Creation. These two primary constituents of the universe are Apsū and Tiamat. The "mingling of the waters" is symbolic of their unity, and they together are thought to constitute the First Dragon, the Abyss, the primal matter of the world. But this also represents their sexual union and the beginning of the cosmic sexual current which underlies the creation of all life in the universe. For this reason, they can be viewed as extension of the Primal Dragon of the Void, or as the first gods torn from the undifferentiated body of the Dragon, the Primal Ocean of Black Waters. As the First Manifestation of the Dragon, Tiamat possesses all the powers of the Mother of Everything. She can "mingle" her waters with the male principle in order to create gods, but she can also conceive monsters and demons by herself, tearing them from her boundless flesh, cloaking them with godlike powers and elevating above all other creations. This is the power that belongs to the First Mother alone. Tiamat is, at the same time, the Primal Dragon, the first cosmic force in itself and the first manifestation of the Dragon. However, in the Mesopotamian lore, the original, formless mass or watery matter was called Apsû, which was later the name of the first male deity, and to whom

---

[7] Samuel Noah Kramer: *Sumerian Mythology*

the mythology attributed the same powers of creation as to the Dragon Goddess Tiamat. Through the Work with Draconian manifestations, gods, demons and other entities, we can access the original power of the Primal Dragon, which is formless, disordered, nameless, and boundless. This is the mystery of the First Mother which is revealed through the rites of her Draconian Alchemy.

Tiamat was slain by Marduk in the battle for the new cosmic order, but she remains slumbering under the foundations of the world, ready to awaken and rise, to shake and devour the creations of gods and the civilizations of man, for she is the one who gives birth to all things and swallows them in the eternal cosmic cycle. Her flesh and bones constitute the structure of the world, her blood flows through the veins of all living beings on the earth, and her primal consciousness dwells at the root of the human mind, reflecting the myth of the Primal Dragon in human biological pattern and in the reptilian origin of human brain stem. She is the Inner Dragon, the Dragon Within, the Serpent Kundalini, which awakens and opens consciousness for the flow of the Ophidian and Draconian currents. She is the force that cannot be tamed or locked within the boundaries of a structured order. Her timeless essence is boundless. She rises from within, lifting the soul beyond the Gates of the Night, where consciousness is shattered in the Womb of Chaos, decomposed and stripped from mundane conditioning. She is the Seducer to the wanderers on the Path of Flames who emblazes the divine spark in their blood. She is the Mother to those who dare to descend into the Heart of Darkness in order to be reborn in her Womb and to rise to the heights of heavens on her flaming wings. And she is also the Destroyer of the weak and the false, those who choose stagnation and ignorance over desire and evolution.

But Tiamat is also the Dragon Without, the fearsome force of Nature. The thunderstorms, the fire in the volcanoes, the ferocity of hurricanes and tornadoes, the destructive force of floods, the sudden terror of lightning – Tiamat wields all the powerful and ominous weather phenomena that have never been tamed by man. Her energy constitutes the magnetic field of the whole planet and flows through the mystical veins of the earth in the form of "dragon lines," or "ley lines," which are believed to connect the power spots (ancient vortices of cosmic energy) or "the chakras of the earth." These vortices resonate with the Dragon energy, which can be tapped by the mind aligned with the Draconian Current, by those who have awakened the primal essence of the Dragon within their consciousness. Man is the Flesh and the Blood of the Dragon. Awareness of this legacy unlocks the gateways within our souls through which we can claim the primal potential, rise up to the stars on the wings of the Dragon, reach out for the Tablets of Destinies and become the Gods incarnate, the supreme rulers of the Universe.

THE BATTLE OF LIGHT AND DARKNESS

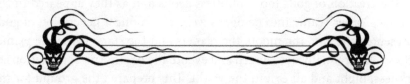

As we already know, in the beginning, nothing existed except the disordered, undifferentiated and boundless mass of primeval waters. Out of this mass, the waters split into the salty ocean of Tiamat and the fresh waters of Apsū, which mingled together and gave birth to first gods: Lahmu and Lahamu, then Anšar (heaven) and Kišar (earth), their son Anu and finally, Nudimmud (Ea), along with other deities of the Babylonian pantheon.

> *"When in the height heaven was not named,*
> *And the earth beneath did not yet bear a name,*
> *And the primeval Apsu, who begat them,*
> *And chaos, Tiamat, the mother of them both*
> *Their waters were mingled together.*
> *And no field was formed, no marsh was to be seen;*
> *When of the gods none had been called into being,*
> *And none bore a name, and no destinies were ordained;*
> *Then were created the gods in the midst of heaven,*
> *Lahmu and Lahamu were called into being.*
> *Ages increased,*
> *Then Anshar and Kishar were created, and over them...*
> *Long were the days, then there came forth;*
> *Anu, their son,*
> *Anshar and Anu*
> *And the god Anu...*
> *Nudimmud, whom his fathers, his begetters,*
> *Abounding in all wisdom,*

He was exceeding strong
He had no rival
Thus were established the great gods."

The creation of gods took countless aeons and as they appeared in the universe, "order" came into being, as well. The younger generation of gods represented the sun, the moon, the planets and the stars, while the primal deities were gradually demonized and eventually became personifications of darkness, night and all evil in the world. This prepared the ground for the legendary struggle between the forces of Light and the powers of Darkness.

In the *Enuma Elish*, the battle takes place when the younger gods slay Apsū, which is the first attempt to gain control over the primeval confusion and disorder. Enraged by the betrayal of her offspring and incited by the other gods, especially Kingu, Tiamat decides to avenge the death of her husband and calls for allies. Her power grows and she creates 11 terrifying monsters, clothed with terror and filled with poison instead of blood. They are fearsome and godlike, embodying the most destructive qualities of the furious Goddess. These 11 monsters are mentioned as vipers, dragons, hurricanes, raging hounds, scorpion-men, mighty tempests, fish-men and rams. Primal gods, such as Lahamu, side with Tiamat and they are included into her army of demons as well. Among the gods, she elevates Kingu, her second husband, to lead the army, and bestows on him the Tablet of Destinies, the supreme dominion over the universe.

"Ummu-Hubur who formed all things,
Made in addition weapons invincible; she spawned monster-
serpents,
Sharp of tooth, and merciless of fang;
With poison, instead of blood, she filled their bodies.
Fierce monster-vipers she clothed with terror,
With splendor she decked them, she made them of lofty stature.
Whoever beheld them, terror overcame him,
Their bodies reared up and none could withstand their attack.
She set up vipers and dragons, and the monster Lahamu,
And hurricanes, and raging hounds, and scorpion-men,
And mighty tempests, and fish-men, and rams;
They bore cruel weapons, without fear of the fight.
Her commands were mighty, none could resist them;

After this fashion, huge of stature, she made eleven [kinds of]
monsters.
Among the gods who were her sons, inasmuch as he had given her
support,
She exalted Kingu; in their midst she raised him to power.
To march before the forces, to lead the host,
To give the battle-signal, to advance to the attack,
To direct the battle, to control the fight,
Unto him she entrusted; in costly raiment she made him sit, saying:
I have uttered thy spell, in the assembly of the gods I have raised thee
to power.
The dominion over all the gods have I entrusted unto him.
Be thou exalted, thou my chosen spouse,
May they magnify thy name over all of them the Anunnaki.
She gave him the Tablets of Destiny, on his breast she laid them,
saying:
Thy command shall not be without avail, and the
word of thy mouth shall be established."

Upon the threat of war, the younger gods are struck by terror and unable to face the forces of Darkness. At first, they try to appease Tiamat, but her fury is too great and they flee at the very sight of her wrath. Then, Ea's son, Marduk, offers to act as the champion of the gods and defeat Tiamat and her allies. Being a solar deity, the greatest of all the powers of Light, Marduk becomes naturally the adversary of the Dragon Goddess and her powers of Darkness. At the great council with a banquet, he proves that he is the worthy to fight on behalf of the gods by demonstrating his creative and destructive powers, and he is given the royal insignia: the sceptre, the throne and the ring. Then, he prepares himself for the fight by taking a bow, a spear and a club. He fills his body with fire and sets the lightning in front of him. He fashions a net with which he intends to catch Tiamat, and he places the four winds near it to prevent her from escaping. He also creates evil winds, tempests and the hurricane to assist him, and finally, mounting his chariot upon the storm with a thunderbolt in his hand, he sets out to face Tiamat. The monsters and fiends are smitten with fear at the mere sight of his power, but Tiamat strikes with spells and incantations. Her attack fails, however, and she is killed and split asunder. Marduk smashes her skull with his club and scatters her blood to the north wind. He catches the 11 monsters in his net and tramples upon their bodies as they lie helpless. He takes the Tablet of Destinies from Kingu, seals it with his own seal and lays it on his own breast.

> *"When he had slain Tiamat, the leader,*
> *Her might was broken, her host was scattered.*
> *And the gods her helpers, who marched by her side,*
> *Trembled, and were afraid, and turned back.*
> *They took to flight to save their lives;*
> *But they were surrounded, so that they could not escape.*
> *He took them captive, he broke their weapons;*
> *In the net they were caught and in the snare they sat down."*

What follows the battle is the act of Creation, the transition from Chaos to Order. Marduk splits the body of Tiamat into two parts. From one half, he fashions the dome of heaven and from the other, he constructs the abode of his father, which he places over the Deep, i.e. Apsū. Between the waters of Tiamat and the newly created world, he places a "bolt" and a "watchman" to ensure that the Primordial Chaos will not threaten the new Order.

> *"He split her up like a flat fish into two halves;*
> *One half of her he established as a covering for heaven.*
> *He fixed a bolt, he stationed a watchman,*
> *And bade them not to let her waters come forth."*

Now, he creates E-šara, the mansion of heaven, the dwelling place of the gods, and he continues the process of Creation by organizing the planets and the stars, regulating the sun and the moon and establishing the calendar. He sets the Signs of the Zodiac and associates each sign with a particular month. Then, however, the gods begin to complain that their existence is barren because they lack worshippers who would build them temples and bring offerings. For this reason, Marduk decides to create a human being. Upon Ea's advice, he chooses to sacrifice one of the gods and use the divine blood for his new creation. At the council of the gods, the choice falls on Kingu, who was the instigator of the fight and who was held captive after the defeat of Tiamat. Marduk kills him and from his blood, the god, Ea, fashions mankind for the service of the gods. Now, the gods who sided with Tiamat and were initially forced into labor for the service of the victorious deities are freed from their work and replaced by man. Babylon is established as the residence of Marduk and he is given 50 names and chosen as the supreme ruler of the world and the king of all the gods. The last part of the epic contains a long praise of the chief god and his glorious accomplishments.

It is worth notice that initially Marduk planned to form man from his own blood mixed with earth. Such account was given by Berossus in the 3rd century BCE in the myth of Bēl (Marduk) and Tiamat. In the Babylonian epic, Marduk also declares to create a "bone" for forming man. It is interesting to note that the Assyrian word for "bone" used in the text (*iṣṣimtu*) is the equivalent of the Hebrew word *eṣem* ("bone"), which is used in the narrative of the creation of woman in *Genesis*.[8] The blood of Bēl was used not only in the creation of man, but also in that of animals. Man, however, was the culmination of Marduk's creative work, even though the original role of humanity seems to be rather dismal and pitiful, as they were created solely for the work of the gods, with no higher purpose whatsoever. In Mesopotamian religious practice, this belief was interpreted in a literal sense and the deities in the temples, likewise the king, were clothed, fed, cared for, etc. by the courtiers and priests. The legend of Marduk served as the foundation of patriarchal religion based on the worship of the solar deity. The representative of the chief god, the king, his consort, children or the "servant gods" all received the service of the rest of mankind.

From magical perspective, however, the key to understand the metaphysical meaning of the myth rests on the motif of primordial Chaos being bound and locked within the structures of the new world Order. Marduk defeated Tiamat and her spawn, but did not destroy them. Instead, he made an attempt to tame and suppress these forces by including them in the newly created structure of the universe. Tiamat's soldiers became his trophies; they were disarmed and several of them became the servants of Marduk and later, came to be recognized as his symbolic animals, like e.g. the *mušuššu* serpent. Tiamat herself became the part of the world as the Living Nature and the embodiment of the "mother earth" concept. The blood of Kingu, demon warrior-god, was believed to flow in humans, its demonic element being bound and dormant. The archfiends of Primordial Chaos became now parts of the cosmic Order.

But the Dragon's breath can still be heard in the whisper of the wind, Draconian fire pulsates in the heart of the earth and the blood of man stirs when the slumbering Serpent shakes in her sleep. And what sleeps can be awakened.

---

[8]   Leonard W. King: *Enuma Elish*

THE ELEVEN DEMON-GODS

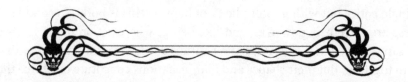

he Hebrew concept of *Tehom,* associated with the Primal Dragon Goddess, in the Qabalah refers to the first of the seven "Infernal Habitations" which correspond to the Qlipoth. The Qlipoth are the "shells," the realm of evil, the dark side of the Qabalistic Tree of Life. They are thought to be the debris left over from an influx of divine force too strong for the Sephiroth to withstand, which had poured out of the Tree and created an anti-world in the dark regions. They are inhabited by demons and malevolent spirits responsible for all evil in the world. The Qlipoth is the anti-structure to the Tree of Sephiroth, and while there are ten Sephiroth to signify the unity and perfection of God, there are eleven qlipoth to disturb the original balance represented by the number 10. The highest qlipha, Thaumiel, which stands in opposition to the divine unity of Kether, is split in two and called the Twin God. Each qlipha represents an adverse aspect of the corresponding sephira and is considered to be its anti-pole. These forces are sometimes identified with the eleven powers of Tiamat and her eleven demons. The whole Tree of Qlipoth is thought to be dark, feminine, and personified by a female deity – most often this is Lilith who acts as the first Adversary and Initiator of mankind, while the primal Dragon Goddess Tiamat, who embodies the very source of the forces of Chaos, exists outside the structures of Creation and beyond emanations of Divine Light.

The eleven monsters of Tiamat are mentioned in the *Enuma Elish,* along with the terms that signify their nature or species, but not exactly their names. In the research literature, they are often treated as such and so, they are presented in this grimoire. Several of these names signify the plural and might refer to a group of entities. Within the rites of magic, these spirits may seem multiple indeed. This is because of their vast, complex and amorphous nature. They are also chaotic and disordered by nature and they may assume a great number of forms and shapes, shifting them within minutes of even seconds, splitting into multiple parts, or manifesting all of them at the same time, which gives an illusory impression that we are not dealing with a single entity but with a multiplicity of beings. This is both true and false. These are extremely powerful, god-like beings who exist on many levels at the same time, and thus, can assume hundreds of forms and manifest all of them together. But their shapes and manifestations constitute one force that should be called as a whole.

From the myth, we learn that they are "sharp of tooth, merciless of fang," their bodies filled with venom instead of blood, "clothed with terror," decked with splendor, god-like and powerful. Whoever beheld them was overcome with terror and none could withstand their attack. They are referred to as "matchless weapons" and enumerated in the following order: vipers and dragons, the monster Lahamu, hurricanes, raging hounds, scorpion-men, mighty tempests, fish-men, and bison-men.

From magical perspective, they constitute the eleven dark and destructive powers of Tiamat and several of them may be also compared to the qlipothic forces of the Qabalistic Tree of Night. However, it would be rather artificial and limited if we tried to fit each of them into a concrete qlipothic level; their powers are too complex and their nature too chaotic to form an initiatory map of spiritual progress, as the Qabalistic Tree is understood by occult practitioners. There is even possibility that the story might be read in a literal way and that the monsters of Tiamat represent particular aspects of spiritual warfare. In the myth, they were created as an army with each of them as a type of weapon. This is also how these primal forces manifest most frequently in rites of magic. Modern practitioners can successfully use them for magical attack and defense, but their dissolving and venomous powers can also be employed in works of initiatory alchemy and used for self-empowerment. It is possible that a few of them might have connection to astrology indeed, which was suggested by historians and researchers of Babylonian magic and mythology. The historical sources, however, are not unanimous in their interpretation of particular creatures – a chosen monster in one book is described with qualities which in another source are attributed to a completely different entity. Also, the results from practical work and magical research confirm the suggested attributes in several cases, but differ considerably in many others. But, then again, we should stress that the usual attributes were attached to the creatures on the basis of linguistic analysis of the words used in the *Enuma Elish*. In this book, we will broaden this perspective and present unknown aspects of the Mighty Eleven, which were lost over the ages but can still be accessed by the modern practitioner.

But, were these entities really lost and their powers forgotten? To answer this question, we have to take a closer look at Mesopotamian myths and legends that follow the original story of Creation. As we already observed, the eleven monsters of Tiamat were bound and included in the new world structure by Marduk, and thus, forced to serve the gods of Light. From then on, they were believed to exist as signs of the Zodiac, as constellations, stellar forces and servants to the gods and guardians of their temples. Yet, there are enough references to demons, evil spirits, malevolent creatures, and un-quiet souls to prove that not all of them were bound and subjected to the rule of the gods. They haunt places where the veil between dimensions is thin, lurking behind the Gates of the Night, lying in wait for the doorways to open and let them into the world of man. They roam across deserts and wastelands, appear in desolate and abandoned sceneries and dwell in the bowels of the earth or on tops of mountains. These dark realms inhabited by demons and monsters are identified with the Qlipoth from Qabalistic legends, the abode of all Evil in the world. These hordes and legions of fiends dwell in the Womb of the Night, between spaces and dimensions, and each day they breed more horrors, waiting to invade the world and to destroy it, so that the Primal Chaos would reign once again.

Ancient mythologies are full of legends of serpents and dragons dwell-ing beneath the earth or among the stars, of primordial beings and entities that existed before the creation of man, of monsters born in the Womb of Chaos. There are also mythological serpents that personify the Primal Cha-os itself, boundless Darkness existing outside the structures of the world, encircling the universe and holding the earth in their timeless coils. The Scandinavian Jormungandr, for instance, coils around Midgard, the world of man, while the Hindu serpent, Sesha, floats in the cosmic ocean, forming the bed of Vishnu, one the supreme gods in the Hindu religion. Sesha is the king of the *Nagas*, who were ancient deities depicted as snakes, primal beings of Creation. It is believed that when the Serpent uncoils, time moves forward and universes are created; when he coils back, worlds cease to exist. A similar function is attributed to the Egyptian serpent, Mehen, who coils around the Sun God, Ra, to protect him on his journey through the Ocean of the Night. He is called the Encircler and believed to be the Most Ancient One, the primal serpent-god who comes from primordial times before the creation of mankind.

Mesopotamian myths and legends contain many references to demons and evil spirits whose nature seems primal, amorphous and chaotic. These spirits are the "wide-spreading clouds which darken the day" and storms and winds that "cannot be withstood." They bring terror and gloom upon the world, wreak havoc and destruction across the fields and slay humans and animals alike. They dwell beneath the Mountain of Sunset, behind the Gates of the Night, in caverns of the earth and in desolate places. They have no name and are "unknown in heaven and earth." In accounts gathered from the tablets, they are mentioned as evil spirits, whirlwinds, hag-demons, plague-gods, ghosts, devils that lie in wait in the desert, bad winds, the Evil Eye that "brings sickness upon men," or demon-harlots who steal the semen to engender demons and haunt the houses of men to make them barren.

From magical perspective, their powers manifest on both macrocosmic and microcosmic level. They are the principles of Primordial Chaos which act against the Divine Order: against Light, laws and regulations, civilization, religions, and the foundations of the world of man. But viewed as the Chaos Within, they also represent dark instincts, hidden lusts and savage urges that are atavistic, primal, inherent in the human soul, but repressed to the utmost regions of consciousness. On the microcosmic level, they are the antinomian impulses which drive man towards individual isolation and self-deification. They are the hurricane of change, initiators of movement and evolution, the divine flame of Becoming, manifestations of the primal Draconian force underlying the whole Creation.

In Mesopotamian lore, however, these demons and evil spirits are also thought to act against man and their destructive powers are believed to cause weakness, diseases and death. They bring headaches, fever, pain, dysentery, tumors, ulcers, leprosy, seizures, and agony. They make men and women barren, slaughter people and tear out their hearts. They can set the house on fire, make crops wither and bring sickness to animals. These descriptions have a great resemblance to the powers of the Mighty Eleven as they are revealed in this grimoire. By means of malevolent magic, they can be bound to do the sorcerer's bidding and to destroy the chosen target. Among works of malediction, the Assyrian formulas given in *Chaldean Magic. Its Origin and Development* list the following manifestations of a demonic attack:

"Painful disease of the bowels,
The infirmity which makes gloomy and cuts...
That which acts in the mouth, the poison noxious to the voice,
The expectoration of the consumption which noxiously prostrates,
Scrofula, pustules, falling off of the nails,
Purulent eruptions, inveterate tetters,
Shingles causing pits and scars,
Leprosy covering the skin,
Food which reduces the body of man to a skeleton,
Food which eaten is returned again,
Liquids which make the drinker swell,
Fatal poison,
The pestilential wind which comes from the desert and returns not,
The frost which makes the earth to shiver,
The excess of heat which makes the skin to crack,
Evil destiny which unexpectedly cuts off a man's career..."

These maledictions and many others are taught by the particular demons of the Mighty Eleven when they are called to manifestation through the rites of evocation. In Akkadian and Assyrian spells, incantations and exorcisms, they are attributed to the works of evil spirits known as Utuq, Alal, Gigim, Telal, Gallu and Maskim. These entities are described as phantoms, spectres, vampires, incubi, succubae, nightmares and spirits that can be bound by wicked sorcery to work evil against another human being. Telal, the bull demon, is possibly a form of Kusarikku, "the bison-man" from the Tiamat legend, but also the other beings are highly reminiscent of the Mighty Eleven. Many of them seem to have primal nature and their work is directed against the cosmic Order. They ravage the heaven and the earth, disturb the stars of the sky and interrupt the movement of planets, producing "the evil command which comes from the midst of heaven; the evil destiny which issues from the depths of the abyss." The whole world trembles at their wickedness and they can even threaten the gods. In exorcisms and incantations, it is usually Marduk, the chief of all gods, who is called to protect man from their malevolent work. One of the incantations, quoted by Francois Lenormant in his *Chaldean Magic*, provides an interesting example of their attack:

"The execrable Idpa acts upon the head of man,
The malevolent Namtar upon the life of man,
The malevolent Utuq, upon the forehead of man,
The malevolent Alal upon the chest of man,
The malevolent Gigim upon the bowels of man,
The malevolent Telal upon the hand of man."

Those beings are believed to be wicked and evil by nature and "bad in themselves." They feed on blood and bow to no gods. They manifest as winds whose burning breath favors the development of diseases, evil spirits of deserts and wilderness who torment mankind, dwellers of bleak summits of mountains, pestilential marshes, and sea demons and monsters. It was thought that "the *Utuq* inhabits the desert, the *Mas* dwells on the heights, the *Gigim* wanders in the desert and the *Telal* steals into towns."[9] Their original abode, however, is the desert and the exorcisms are used to send them back to their place of habitation. The desert in the lore of the Middle East seems to represent the original Abyss, the birthplace and the abode of all demons and evil spirits of the world.

A popular practice in Mesopotamia was to avert the bad influence of one demon by using a talisman or a statue of another. Hence, the images and sculptures of demons and monstrous beasts were placed on the doors, above entrances and by the sides of the gates. It was also believed that those guardians were real spirits, bound by spells and magic of the gods. Such was the case of human-headed bulls that guarded the gateway to infernal regions at the Mountain of Sunset. According to the same belief, demons or genii watched over heavenly spheres and boundaries between the realm of Divine Order and the primordial Ocean of Chaos which existed outside the world created by the gods. These divine guardians were: the Sed, who was depicted as a bull with a human face, the Lamas, who was a lion with a man's head, the Ustur, pictured in a human form and the Nattig, with the head of an eagle. In the Western lore, these entities would be later preserved as four symbolic creatures supporting the throne of Jehova, in the form of the so-called "tetramorph."

Monsters and demons served as guardians of temples and were depicted on the doors, placed as statues or carved on the walls, plagues, cylinders and decorations. In the Sumerian temple of E-ninnû, there were ornaments

---

9 Francois Lenormant: *Chaldean Magic. Its Origin and Development*

on the door in the shape of *idim* (*uridimmu*), or "raging lions;" *muš-ša-tur* (*bašmu*), i.e. "serpents;" and *muš-huš*, "terrible vipers and monsters." Clay plaques from Akkadian period contain depictions of gods fighting monsters and demons, such as fiery Cyclopes, dragons, serpents, lions, dragon-serpents, winged beasts, etc. However, the primordial monsters were often depicted as companions, servants and guardians of the gods. The boundary-stones (*kudurru*) are the most characteristic monuments from the Kassite period and they show Mušuššu, for example, as the dragon of Marduk, and the goat-fish (which is probably a reference to Kulullû) as the symbolic animal of the god, Ea. In depictions from the post-Kassite Babylonia, we can also see the bull and the lightning (the bull might refer to Kusarikku and the lightning bolt was symbolic of the weather demons) as the emblems of the storm Adad. The epithet of Adad was also "the great radiant bull" and he was pictured as a warrior wearing a helmet with bull horns, possibly an attribute acquired from the primordial demon-god, Kusarikku. Bulls, dragons and lions also appeared as ornaments on Nebuchadrezzar's Ishtar Gate in Babylon, along the Processional Way, constructed in the 6th century BCE. Mušuššu, who became the "dragon of Marduk," was usually depicted as a hybrid creature that was scaly-coated with the head bearing the double horns of the Arabian horned viper. The front legs of the creature were feline, the hind legs resembled the limbs of a bird of prey and the tail terminated in a scorpion sting.[10]

It is also worth noticing that the scorpion-man was a popular entity in Babylonia and Assyria. It was often depicted on reliefs, as well as on boundary-stones, the most famous of which is the image of the creature that had the torso, head and arms of a human, the lower body of a scorpion and was aiming with a bow and arrow. Scorpion-men were popular guardians and openers of the way to the Underworld. In the legend of Gilgamesh, they guarded the gates to the land of the Kur at the mountains of Mashu through which the Sun God, Shamash, traveled at night. They are demonic and fearsome. Their heads touch the sky and their glance is death. The scorpion was also the symbol of the goddess, Ishkhara, and represented the constellation and the Zodiac sign of Scorpio. Ishkhara was sometimes described as the scorpion goddess herself, or many-breasted Mother Scorpion who dwelt among the stars and nourished the souls of the dead with the milk from her breasts. Her sacred animals were the scorpion and the dragon.

---

[10] Joan Oates: *Babylon*

But, there are also deities whose nature and attributes reflect the Draconian aspects of the Primal Chaos, the First Dragon Goddess. Among those worthy of special note is the goddess Nintu, sometimes identified with Ninhursag, who is associated with the creation of man from clay and blood. The number of votive figures offered to her by women who desired offspring suggests that among the people of Mesopotamia she occupied the position of the Mother Goddess. She was depicted with an elaborate tiara and veil, with a garment covering her loins, but she was uncovered above the waist and sometimes, she was pictured as suckling a child at the left breast. The upper part of her body was that of a naked woman and the lower part was scaly, like the skin of a snake, which represented her primal Draconian origin. It is interesting to note that the form of a half-woman half-snake is also often encountered among manifestations of serpent demons that belong to the eleven monsters of Tiamat. These entities usually appear in the female form, with snake or dragon scales, or with reptilian parts of the body. Nintu is possibly one of these primordial creatures, born in the Womb of Primal Chaos but incorporated into the Babylonian pantheon and the new religious structure.

The attributes of Tiamat, the First Mother, were also preserved in powers and attributes of other female goddesses, such as Ninhursag, Namtu, Belit or Ishtar. The Akkadian Belit, or Belit-lli also goes by "Lady of the Gods," "Lady of the Lower Abyss," "Mother of the Gods," "Queen of the Earth" and "Queen of Fertility." These titles and functions belong to her, as well as to the other female deities who evolved on the concept of primordial humidity, which was the source of all life, originally called *Tamti*, the sea."[11] And even though there are many exorcisms of evil spirits in Mesopotamian lore, there exists no exorcism of Tiamat, the Primal Dragon. She is the natural and indispensable part of the universe, and she cannot be banished, for the world would cease to exist without the Dragon force that constitutes the flesh and the soul of all living beings. She is believed to sleep below the surface of the earth, not dead but dormant, powerful, primal, fearsome and very real. Her powers can be tapped and accessed by those who do not fear to open the Gates of the Night and to walk through, those "who are skillful to rouse Leviathan."[12]

---

[11] Francois Lenormant: *Chaldean Magic. Its Origin and Development*
[12] Job 3:8

The description of Nintu is quoted in R. Campbell Thomson's *Devils and Evil Spirits of Babylonia,* alongside references to other gods and demons whose appearance reveals their Draconian origin. Among those beings, the author mentions a creature whose head is that of a serpent, ears like those of a basilisk, horns twisted into three curls, and the base of his feet are claws. His name is *Sassu-urinnu* and he is a sea monster, "a form of Ea," which means that he probably comes from the primeval ocean of Apsū, or perhaps is one of the primordial beings born in the Womb of Tiamat. Another description refers to a female entity whose name is unknown, as it was not preserved on the tablets, but who is "the chosen of Ereshkigal." She has the horns of a gazelle, one of which is bent over her back and the other grows straight over her face. She has the ear of a sheep, the fist of a man and the body of a fish with snake scales. Another nameless god mentioned on the same tablets has the face of a man, horns of an ox, wings of a bird and the body of a lion. There is also a being named *Laḥmu ippiru,* with the tail of a lion and a body of a *kissugu,* who touches heaven and earth with his hands and legs. The primordial god, Lahamu, is described here, as well and he is depicted as a man from the waist to the loins. From the loins to the feet, he is a dog, and he has the wings of a bird, ears of an ox and a horn on his head. He also wears a headband and he is clothed with a doublet on his breast. The remaining descriptions refer to a god named Šulul, who has the face of a man and the body of a fish, *Niziḳtum,* who has the body of a naked woman and wings of a bird and a nameless goddess with a human body and the head of bird, while she wears a veil hanging from her head to her shoulders and two torches in her hands. These bestial parts of the body suggest the primal nature of the entities and they are also parts of the primordial demons of Tiamat. Snake heads, scale-covered bodies, claws and talons, fish parts and bird wings – these are all common attributes of the Mighty Eleven and manifestations of the Primal Chaos.

The most popular theory in the source literature on the myth of Creation, however, is that the primordial monsters and god-like beings became the Babylonian Zodiac. E.A. Wallis Budge, in his book, *Amulets and Superstitions,* claims that the Signs of the Zodiac were none other than: Ummu-Khubur, i.e. Tiamat, Kingu (her husband), the Viper, the Snake, Lakhamu, the Whirlwind, the Ravening Dog, the Scorpion-Man, the Hurricane, the Fish-Man, the Horned Beast (Capricorn), and the Weapon (Thunderbolt). In other words, these were the creatures originally created by Tiamat to fight in the war, including the demon-god Kingu and the Dragon Goddess, herself. This theory is based on conviction that the Signs of the Zodiac set up by Marduk were different from the old ones and replaced a system which pre-existed the rise of civilization founded on the laws of patriarchal religion. The new Signs were as follows: the Labourer (Goat), the Star and the Bull of Heaven (Bull), the Faithful Shepherd of Heaven and the Great Twins (Twins), Tortoise (Crab), Great Dog/Lion (Lion), Virgin with ear of corn (Virgo), Zibanitum (Scales), Aḵrabu (Scorpion), the god Enurta (Bow), the Goat-Fish (Capricorn), the Great Star (Water-bearer), and the Star and the Band of Fishes (the Fishes).

The majority of knowledge about Mesopotamian demons is generally based on incantations, hymns, formulas and exorcisms against evil spirits, who continuously attempt to destroy the safety of man and bring Darkness and Chaos into the world. These conjurations were designed to threat away the demons, to avert their actions and to protect man from their attacks. Among them, we find a long and suggestive incantation against the seven malevolent demons called the Maskim. The formula was translated into English by R. Campbell Thompson and published in 1903 in the book, *The Devils and Evil Spirits of Babylonia*. The Maskim were the Ensnarers, the layers of ambushes and the most wicked demons that surpassed all others in power and evil. On clay tablets, they are described as "ruthless spirits created in the vault of heaven," but their nature seems dark and primal. This might suggest that they were originally demons of Primordial Chaos who, while bound within the new structures of the world, had power that was too great to withstand, allowing them to break free and wreak havoc across the land. Their descriptions resemble the nature and attributes of the Mighty Eleven from the Creation myth, and they were the most feared evil spirits in the Mesopotamian lore. Even though they are sometimes referred to as "the messengers of Anu," the Sky God, manifesting as flashes of lightning, they were believed to be the creatures of the Underworld, chthonic entities residing in the bowels of the earth. But, there are also accounts which state that the number of the Maskim was "twice seven" – "seven in heaven, seven on earth." Therefore, they seemed to constitute two distinct groups of spirits, both destructive and terrifying. While the seven chthonic demons caused plagues and disasters on the earth (earthquakes, floods, etc.), the sky spirits manifested as raging storms, hurricanes, bolts of lightning and destructive winds that brought "darkness in heaven" and "cast gloom over the bright day."

Like the primordial monsters of Tiamat, they were amorphous and complex, without shape or form, neither male, nor female. Described as destructive storms and evil winds, they rushed like a flood over the earth. "From the four corners, the thrust of their advance burns like fire, they violently invade the dwellings of man, they lay bare the town as well as the country." No door could shut them out, no bolt turned them back. They dashed along from house to house and glided through each door. They embodied the force of Chaos and opposed the natural course of nature. The first was "the South wind;" the second – "a dragon, whose mouth is opened... that none can measure;" the third – "a grim leopard, which carries off the young;" the fourth– "a terrible Shibbu;" the fifth–"a furious Wolf, who knoweth not to flee;" the sixth–"a rampant ... which marches against god and king;" and the seventh was "a storm, an evil wind, which takes vengeance." As these descriptions match the attributes of the Mighty Eleven, they seem to be related to the original Children of Tiamat, or they can even be the primordial demons themselves, manifesting their powers in the new structures of the world.

The accounts from the tablets depict the Maskim as messengers of Namtar and the throne-bearers of Ereshkigal, which points at their connection to the Underworld. Ereshkigal is the Queen of the Great Below, the goddess who rules the land of the dead, together with her consort Nergal. Namtar is her messenger and minister, one of the demons of the nether regions, the bringer of death. His name means "destiny" or "death." He was believed to command sixty diseases in the form of demons that afflicted different parts of human body. Namtar was also the personification of the plague and together with *Idpa*, the fever, they were considered as two of the most formidable demons who afflicted mankind.

According to the legend, the Maskim were born out of Anu, together with other main deities, and are equally ancient. They are alternately referred to as gods, demons and spirits. Their ally is the Imkhullu, "the evil wind," and their main enemy is the God of Fire, together with other leading deities: Enlil, Ea, and Ishtar. The Maskim were created "to wreak destruction." In order to avoid it, the gods divided the whole heaven among the three of them: Sin, God of the Moon, Shamash, God of the Sun, and Ishtar, Mistress of Heavens, daughter to Sin and sister to Shamash. But the seven evil gods stormed the vault of heaven and brought onto their side Sin, Shamash and Adad, the God of Storms. They darkened the moon by an eclipse and brought thick clouds to cover the sun. Darkness fell upon the earth. Neither the moon nor the sun was shining. The gods were terrified and called for Marduk, the God of War, to fight the demons. Many fragments of the legend are missing, but what is left gives a powerful account of the nature of the seven demons who managed to threaten the whole Divine Order. They could ravage heaven and earth, interrupt the movement of the stars and darken the sun and the moon. The gods' efforts to oppose them were futile. Even the powerful God of Fire was helpless in the face of their powers.

Descriptions of the Maskim are highly evocative of the original eleven demons, as well. They are dragons and serpents, storms and raging winds, wolves and wild beasts dwelling in desolate places. The demon of the South wind, who is the first of the Maskim, is connected with the desert, the heat of the sun and the drought which brings death to humans and animals alike, causing diseases and destruction of crops. It is an extremely hot wind, burning everything that it encounters on its way, like a black, demonic fire or a destructive tornado. In ancient Mesopotamia, winds and hurricanes were often regarded as demons, usually elemental ones. Sometimes, they were believed to be messengers sent by gods to punish humans for their sins. The demon of the South wind assumes many forms or appears completely formless: as a whirlpool of black dust. When he manifests, he comes as anthropomorphic lizard-like figure with long hair and two pairs of wings; as a man with a demonic face and long fiery hair; or as a black shape wearing a mask on the face. He is the black wind of the desert, carving pictures and glyphs on the desert sand, blood-red in the light of the setting sun, marking the entrance to the Underworld. He emerges from dark pits of the earth and guides the wanderers into underground labyrinths, temples, and tunnels. There, the black fire burns so fiercely that one can hardly find any air to breathe and the heat burns the body and releases the spirit, transforming the Initiate into a living torch or a fire elemental. Similar destructive force is attributed to another of the Maskim demons: "a storm, an evil wind which takes vengeance." This spirit reveals a close connection to violent forces of nature as well: storms, hurricanes, tornadoes, heavy rains, thunder and lightning, i.e. all fierce phenomena which belong to the sphere of air. He appears to the conjuror in the form of a black winged figure or as an airy serpent with human head and horns. He may also manifest as a destructive power of nature: a violent wind that tears trees out of the ground, collapses buildings, and destroys everything on his way. He enters the Temple like a hurricane, lifting the soul beyond the Gates of the Night, raising storms and causing severe damage to the enemies. There is also a demon who personifies the very essence of Chaos and Disorder, a mysterious being who "marches against god and king," spirit of rebellion against artificial structures established by humans and their gods. The demon himself is extremely chaotic and assumes hundreds of shapes. However, none of them is permanent and each form is continuously shifting into another. Sometimes, he resembles a tiger, a panther, a werewolf or he might simply consist of many animal parts, as if he embodied all beasts of prey at the same time. He is the beast rising from the Black Waters of Tiamat in order to tear the world apart, destroying the Divine Order and bringing the Current of Primal Chaos onto the earth. The spirit also has necromantic associations; he may manifest as a destructive force of death that does not spare anyone – neither kings nor gods. As we learn from mythological accounts, in Mesopotamia, even gods could die, e.g. Gugal-Ana, the first husband of the goddess, Ereshkigal, died and later, she married her second consort, Nergal. Thus, the force of the demon is not only the principle of cosmic rebellion, but also death, which falls upon living beings, as well as human civilizations.

The Maskim also include the demons in the form of dragons and serpents. One of them is the dragon "whose mouth is opened ... that none can measure." The other is "a terrible Shibbu," which, in Akkadian, means "serpent." Dragon-like creatures in ancient Mesopotamia were not always viewed as demonic. In the Sumerian poetry, there is a term *ušumgal* (a serpent monster), which does not have any pejorative meaning, but denotes a powerful god or a glorious king, and possibly refers to one of Tiamat's monsters, the entity named Ušumgallu, who became associated with royal powers in the new structure of the world. In myths and legends, we encounter many dragon and serpent creatures, e.g. the serpent-dragon (Mušhuššu), or the lion-dragon (Asag or Anzu). As we have already observed, Mušhuššu was a symbol of divine authority over the Primal Chaos represented by the Dragon, and he was associated with such gods as Marduk, Nabu, or Ašur. But, then again, Asag and Anzu were vicious demons, bringing plagues and disasters upon mankind. The nature of the Maskim dragon-demon also seems ambiguous. He assumes forms and shapes connected to all elements. He can become a water serpent-dragon, like Leviathan, with his jaws as the waves of the ocean. But, he also manifests as a fiery dragon, with electric and fiery breath, casting lightning with his fearsome eyes. Furthermore, he can be wholly chthonic and appear as a part of the earth or the Underworld. His head is a huge mountain and his open jaws form an entrance to the cave with sharp stones and rocks resembling the teeth of a beast. His flesh is the earth itself with its underground caves, labyrinths and temples. His blood constitutes underground rivers, filled with water that looks like blood in the dim light of the Underworld. This form might be connected with Mušmah-hu, another entity from the Mighty Eleven. And finally, the demon may also assume an airy form. In this shape, he appears as a huge cosmic dragon, encircling the whole universe, like Ouroboros serpent. His jaws are so vast that he could easily swallow the world. His body is the night sky and his scales are the stars shining bright on the firmament. All these shapes point at the universal nature of the Dragon, the primal force that contains all four elements within, binding them with the fifth one: the Spirit. The entity also seems to unite the powers and attributes of the dragon and serpent creatures from the original myth of Creation. The remaining powers are attributed to Shibbu, the demon depicted as a snake with a pair of horns. This depiction possibly refers to Bašmu from the Tiamat legend, but it can also be applied to powers and attributes of other serpent creatures born in the Womb of Chaos. From magical perspective, this Maskim spirit resembles Mušhuššu, as they both tend to appear as shadowy, ghastly spectres, spitting out deadly venom. They coil around the Initiate and bite him, plunging their teeth into mortal flesh and infecting the soul with poisonous substance. And as the venom flows through the veins, the Initiates fall into hallucinogenic trance and through vapors of greenish smoke, they experience visions of serpents and vipers, serpent-people, underground temples with serpent statues, and endless tunnels, writhing and pulsating, as if they were alive. There, in the bowels of the earth, they meet dwellers of the Underworld – half-human half-serpents ruled by the Snake Goddess. They would invite the wanderers to immerse in the cauldron filled with green venom which induces further visions and hallucinations, through which the Initiate is transformed into serpent in order to glide between worlds, dimensions and angles. The magical power of this Maskim demon is the art of bestial shape-shifting into the form of a serpent through the trance of hallucinatory intoxication with the venomous *elixir vitae*. The energy of the demon is also very vampiric in its nature and apart from self-initiatory purposes, it could be used in astral vampirism where the victim would be poisoned and drained of his astral energy through the form of this shadowy wraith.

Finally, there were also demons in the form of wild beasts, wolves, leopards, lions, etc. These entities are highly reminiscent of the eleven monsters of Tiamat, as well. One of such characters in the Mesopotamian lore is "a grim leopard which carries off the young," also one of the Maskim group. This spirit embodies atavistic instincts of savage hunt. Leopard is an emblem of the wild predator, shadow demon which hunts under the cloak of the night, searching for prey, and such is the influence of the demon on the consciousness of the Initiate. Human instincts are left behind and one experiences a drive of primal animal impulses, evoking visions of running through the woods and wilderness in search of prey, violent killing, the greedy devouring of the flesh and drinking of the blood, as if driven by a primal urge to satisfy the hunger. The leopard demon is the animal spirit worshipped by bloody cults in which people dressed in leopard skins and masks and dancing in a wild fashion around an altar with a freshly captured prey, perform the act of ritual cannibalism. The practice of wearing animal skins is typical of many African tribes. In Nigeria, this custom is cultivated in funeral ceremonies, when the deceased are dressed in leopard skins. Similar practices were also used in funeral rites of ancient Egypt. In Mesopotamia, the custom of wearing animal skins was not unknown either. On ancient reliefs, we can often see people dressed in lion skins, embodying the powers of the animal. Bestial disguise was a symbolic acquirement of the animal skills, strength and agility. In magical practice, it replaces the art of shape-shifting on the mundane level. It induces a particular kind of trance which allows for moving onto the astral level and for a complete transformation into a beast – a manifestation of one's hidden instincts and lusts. In this case, it is the manifestation of atavistic predatory instincts, which become awakened by absorption of this dark energy. But, there is also another entity among the Maskim who embodies the concept of a spiritual predator. It is "a furious wolf who knoweth not to flee." This being has a close connection to the concept of lycanthropy, shamanism, nagualism and totem animals. The demon appears as a huge wolf or an anthropomorphic werewolf, with sharp teeth and hard claws, which might have been inspired by the picture of Uridimmu, the entity from the Tiamat myth, who manifests in lupine or canine shapes on occasion. He haunts his prey, eats the flesh of his victims and drinks their fresh, warm blood. In rites of invocation, he also reveals to the Initiate the secret of transformation, under the light of the full moon, in severe pain which tears apart the mundane flesh and releases the soul – the bestial/animal element inherent in human DNA. This concept of bestial soul is rooted in shamanic beliefs in totem animals, guardian spirits and guides through spiritual realms. In various parts of the world, it was known as the *nagual*, or the *fylgia*, and in witchcraft, as the familiar spirit of a witch. Like the leopard demon, this Maskim spirit represents the art of therianthropy, which has a long tradition worldwide in many cultures and their mythologies and especially in magical customs. To transform oneself into a desired animal, practitioners of these ancient rites dressed themselves in animal skins, rubbed their bodies with magic ointments, drank water out of animal's footprints, or used a wide range of magical spells and incantations. It was believed that by these practices one may acquire skills and qualities of the animal. When the transformation and mental identification was complete, man was believed to become a savage and cruel animal – a werewolf in which all human instincts were replaced by bestial. In the form of a beast of prey, the Initiate roamed across woods and wilderness, killing men and animals encountered on his way in order to satisfy his primal hunger lust for ultimate freedom from all constraints of mundane reality. This flight of the soul in unrestrained liberation from the flesh is the essence of the Mighty Eleven. It is the ascent to the Gates of Flesh and beyond, through the Gates of the Night into the Womb of the Dragon, when the soul is dissolved, reborn and fortified by the primal Draconian force of the First Mother.

BOOK 2

THE CHILDREN
OF TIAMAT

METHODS OF WORK

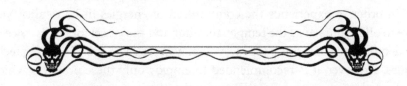

Before starting the Work with the spirits presented in this grimoire, it is necessary to get familiar with the basic tools and methods needed for the rituals. Techniques described here are specific for this Gnosis, but they can also be used in other magical workings. Draconian magic is personal, dynamic, versatile, elevating individual experience over fixed structures and established traditions. It is its nature to challenge, question, destroy and create anew. Methods of Work presented in this book are but a one way to work with this Gnosis, and in fact, there are as many approaches as there are practitioners. This is how the Current remains alive and the primal essence of the Dragon is ever present in the world and within human consciousness, the microcosmic reflection of the Universe. Therefore, the Gnosis that was revealed during the Work with Tiamat and her Children should spread and flourish among those who seek the knowledge and power of the primal Draconian gods. In the present Aeon of Re-Awakening, when the Dragon arises from the Abyss of Oblivion, man should not be afraid to claim the ancient potential and to rise to the stars as well.

INVOCATIONS

In rites of invocation, the essence of the spirits is summoned into the Temple of Flesh. It rises from within in consuming waves of energy, which feels ecstatic and overwhelming. Natural defenses are crushed and annihilated by the dissolving nature of these primal entities. The ego is dissolved and what remains is the raw ecstasy of the soul which is taken beyond the gates of flesh, decomposed and reborn in the Womb of Tiamat, from which it rises purified and empowered by the Black Fire of the Dragon Goddess. The nature of Tiamat's Children is primal and amorphous. Their tendrils will pierce your body from within, like bolts of lightning, penetrating spiritual centers and inflaming them with Draconian energy. The possession is often painful and sexual, the bitter-sweet mixture of agony and pleasure.

In order to experience the communion of energies in its totality, you have to offer yourself as the temple, the altar and the vessel for the essence of the demon-gods. For this purpose, you may use certain ego-dissolving techniques. However, it is recommended to employ only these practices which heighten the senses and open them for the absorption of energies, such as sexual ecstasy. Sexual energies are an excellent vehicle for the essence of Draconian entities which are ever hungry for spiritual substance. All sorts of sexual techniques, from basic auto-erotic practices to advanced sado-masochistic rites, will provide suitable conditions for the shift of consciousness which will take the soul to the boundaries of exhaustion and beyond, into the Womb of the Dragon. Blood is a perfect medium, as well, for the force of the Dragon is contained within the vital-essence and it is the key to the gates of the soul. Bloodletting, however, depletes the organism and it is recommended to use only as much life-substance, as it is absolutely necessary to open the inner and the outer gateways and to provide a channel for the entities to manifest. You should also avoid mind-altering substances, such as alcohol, drugs, hallucinogens, etc. While these methods prove useful in a wide spectrum of magical workings, in this specific type of Gnosis, they will only numb your consciousness and limit the experience. The primal, transformative essence of Draconian gods is enough in itself to take the soul beyond the body and to elevate it in pure ecstasy of possession.

Both in rites of invocation and evocation, the key to the gates of flesh and soul is the blood of the practitioner, the primal substance of the Dragon, the legacy of the Demon-God Kingu. It is the very essence of the Gnosis and the foremost tool of sorcery and spiritual alchemy. Rites of invocation are opened with blood placed on the ritual blade and used to activate the seals. With the blooded ritual blade, you open the Gates of the Night by tracing the glyph of the Key to draw the Current of the Dragon into the Temple. Blood is also required by the gods to manifest, both within and without. Spirits are called by chanting their names and focusing the mind on their seals which should also be drawn or traced with blood. You may wish to prepare the seals prior to the workings, with the blood mixed with paint or ink, but it is strongly recommended that you also trace the lines of the glyphs with blood during the ritual itself. Vital substance is more powerful when imbued with the Essence of Tiamat, the primal Draconian spark which is awakened and ignited in the preliminary invocation of the Dragon.

The gates of flesh, once open, cannot be closed again. The invoked energies will transform you from within, rebuilding and restructuring your spiritual centers, forever merging with your soul. When you open yourself to the primal Current of the Dragon, it will flow into your life, changing it from the very foundations. Energies summoned in rites of invocation can be used for protection and empowerment as well as for destruction and malediction. The powers of gods and spirits manifesting from within are yours to commands and can be directed upon a target. You may choose to use them for self-initiatory purposes, such as to fortify your spiritual body, build protective shields around yourself, open your inner eyes and strengthen your inner vision or transform your consciousness through the alchemy of the soul. But, these energies can also be channeled and directed upon another person, either for protective purposes or in works of hostile sorcery. The Children of Tiamat are very powerful carriers of death energies, ill-wishing and harmful magic. They are bringers of misfortune, weakness and disease. And they are also ruthless vampires, feeding on the life-force of the target, draining it until there is nothing left and the body becomes but an empty shell. However, they are also very chaotic and amorphous, which makes them difficult to focus and control. Effects of destructive magic delivered by these entities manifest upon the victim and in the immediate surroundings. In other words, they will hit not only the target but also every living being around. If you are not powerful enough to control and direct this force, they may easily strike you as well. Another thing that has to be taken into consideration is that these energies strongly affect your consciousness and your perception of the world. They are seductive and they incite the desire and enjoyment of all that is abhorred, disgusting and forbidden. What seems repulsive, becomes exciting, and in rites of possession, when your soul merges with their corrupting essence, you become perfectly capable of things you would normally never do in your mundane life. Human consciousness is left aside and you *become* the primal being yourself. This is an experience that can easily drive a weak mind to madness and obsessions. This Gnosis is not for everyone. It is not for dabblers, disbelievers, pretenders, the feeble-minded, the petty, or the faint-hearted. It is for those who seek genuine power, elevation and evolution of the soul.

EVOCATIONS

In works of evocation the spirits are called to manifest in visible form through a chosen medium, within the area that serves as a focal point for the energies. In these specific rites, the medium is the smoke of the incense and the area of manifestation is the mirror. The essence of the Children of Tiamat, however, is too vast to be enclosed within any particular space, and it is more likely that you will observe their manifestations in the whole ritual room. They can make their initial appearance in the mirror and then assume a visible shape from the thick incense smoke, or they can simply flow through the mirror gateway and manifest above the altar or in any other place in the Temple. But, they rarely stay within the gate itself until the end of the ritual. Protective circles are useless. There are no boundaries that would withhold these powerful entities. The only protection against their overwhelming essence and possible harm is the Draconian Fire, which is ignited by the Invocation of the Dragon and which burns within the soul of the conjuror. It is strongly advised to open all magical operations described in this book with the invocation of Dragon's power and to work in possession with this primal force itself. The Invocation of Dragon can be replaced by the invocation of Tiamat and merging with her boundless essence, or by the invocation of Kingu, who is the lord and commander of all primal beings and stands above the Mighty Eleven.

The primal demon-gods are amorphous in their nature and they can assume any shape or form. Sometimes they come as a shapeless mass of tentacles, heads and eyes, and have to be specifically asked to appear in a form suitable for communication and more pleasing to human senses. They also need a great amount of energy to manifest. For this reason, an offering of either blood or sexual fluids is necessary, and often it is the combination of both. It is natural to feel drained and exhausted, to smaller or larger extent, after the ritual of evocation, and the only way to avoid it is to offer a sacrifice of a living being. This is a controversial practice, which is shunned by many practitioners and it is left to individual choice whether to include it in the Work or not. The sacrifice is not essential for the demon-gods to manifest and convey their Gnosis, but a few of them may openly ask for an offering of life, large quantities of blood or specific bodily organs to be given to them in order to continue the Work. You have to be aware of this before you call these entities to come and do your bidding.

Communication with the demon-gods occurs within the inner mind, though a few of them may also wish to speak to you by verbal means or convey their messages through sigils, glyphs and visual imagery. They also often come with tangible physical phenomena, sounds, scents and tastes. The temperature in the Temple changes and the air becomes electrified. They reveal the secrets of the Nightside and can be asked to serve as guides on the journeys beyond the Gates of the Night. They teach the art of astral shape-shifting and show how to fortify the spiritual body and build powerful defenses. They can also deliver a curse, disease or an attack upon a chosen target. Characteristics of the spirits provided in this grimoire include descriptions of their powers and records of their practical application in self-initiatory alchemy and in the works of malediction.

The formula of calling includes activating the seals with blood, summoning the spirits by chanting their names, providing the substance for manifestation by offering sexual fluids or life energies, reciting the words of a spoken conjuration, scrying for visions of the entities through the mirror and communicating with them about the intent of the rite. The spirits may ask for additional sacrifices or offerings before they bestow on you their gifts. This has to be done in order to continue the operation. After the ritual, you should thank the spirits for coming and dismiss them in the name of the Dragon.

DREAMWORK

The eternal Waters of Tiamat can also be accessed through the doors of sleep. Dreams are manifestations of the unconscious and in dreaming state, we can travel through the Gates of the Night and explore forgotten realms which lie beyond the world of waking. This Work needs advanced skills of dream control and the knowledge of travelling beyond the gates of flesh in comatose lucidity. With the proper practice and systematic training, however, the realm of Dreamlands becomes accessible to any devoted practitioner.

This grimoire provides a simple method of travelling through the door of sleep, which can be applied to all eleven demon-gods, and which only requires basic skills of meditation, affirmation, and visualization. However, if you have enough skill and prior practice in shaping your dreams, it will be easier for you to embark on these journeys and to profit from them.

Before going to sleep, prepare the seal of the chosen spirit, empower it with your own blood if you wish, and focus on it for a while, chanting the name of the demon at the same time. Feel how your inner mind is being connected through the Gates of the Night with the essence of the spirit, and when you sense that the entity is present in the chamber of operation (it is strongly recommended to perform the dreamwork in the room which serves as the Temple for the other rituals), trace the Key of the Night in front of you to empower the flow of energies and speak the words of dream invocation. Place the sigil below the pillow and lie down, visualizing a door with the seal inscribed upon its surface. As the seal comes alive, let the door of sleep open for you to walk through. In descriptions of the demon-gods, you will find suitable visual meditations which you can use to induce dreams inspired by the chosen spirit. If you are an advanced dream traveler, you may wish to call the spirit and simply let it take you on the journey, without following the suggested meditation. In either case, keep your mind focused on the intent to continue the vision in a dream and explore the forgotten realms behind the Gates of the Night.

THE GATES OF THE NIGHT

The Current of the Dragon Goddess Tiamat can be accessed through the gateways to the Nightside which are hidden from the eyes of the profane, but can be opened by those who seek this primal Gnosis. These gates appear when you invoke the Dragon energy into the Temple of Flesh. As the Draconian force of the Kundalini Serpent rises from the base of your spine, ascending through the spinal column and activating spiritual centers, The Eye of the Dragon opens within your inner mind and the illusions of perception are shattered. Then, with your inner eyes, you can see cracks in the surrounding reality, black holes, strangely-looking doors and windows or spots that shine with energy. These portals are the Gates of the Night which connect the Nightside realm with your inner mind. When they are opened, you can travel through these gateways, in between worlds and dimensions, floating with the primal Draconian Current, into the Heart of Darkness, the Womb of Tiamat, the primordial source of all life and all manifestation. In the same way the Current flows through the Gates of the Night into the Temple, the ritual space in which the operation is conducted. This flow of Draconian energies empowers the Temple, fortifies its protections, and provides the energy for the entities of the Nightside to arise and take form on the physical plane. Also, spirits and gods summoned through the rites of magic come through the Gates of the Night in order to manifest in the Temple or within your consciousness.

THE KEY OF THE NIGHT

Provided below is the Key which opens the Gates of the Night and illuminates the dark paths of the Nightside. In the blackness of the Void, which is the Womb of the Dragon Goddess, it shines as a torch, ignited by the inner fire of the soul who travels through the gates of flesh. It is the source of light and the guiding flame on the Path of the Dragon. The eye in the glyph represents the Eye of the Dragon that sees through veils and illusions. The trident is symbolic of the origin of the Current and the primal gods who were created by the First Dragon of the Void.

The Key of the Night is drawn whenever you need to open the outer or the inner gateways. It should be used both in rites of invocation and when you evoke the spirits into visible manifestation. It also opens the gates to Dreamlands and lifts the Veil of the Night as you leave the world of waking. It is traced with a ritual blade covered with practitioner's blood which is empowered by the invocation of the Dragon's force. It is the Blood of the Dragon, which is contained within the Blood of Man, that opens the Gates of the Night and conjoins the worlds within with the worlds without.

The Key should be traced in the ether above the altar, which serves as a focal point for the energies or in the center of a gateway, which you wish to open. Envision how the Key shines and draws the energies of the Nightside into the Temple. Watch the Gates of the Night open in your ritual space and in your inner mind. Feel how the Draconian energies of the Other Side flow into your soul and merge with your consciousness. Let the Key shine as a guiding star on your journeys to the realm of the Nightside, the birthplace of gods. Ignited with the inner flame of your Desire, it burns at the crossroads of the worlds and can be used to open the paths of spiritual evolution.

THE QLIPOTHIC STAR

The Qlipothic Star holds the power of all Children of Tiamat. It is composed of seals of the eleven demon-gods, with the Key of the Night in the center. It is the key to unlocking the power of the Draconian Current within the chamber of operation. The Star should be inscribed with golden colors upon a black surface. It needs a solid material, such as wood, in order to earth the Current on the physical plane. It is specifically needed for certain rites but it should be also placed on the altar or above, to keep the energies flowing and empowering the Temple. After the ritual it should be covered with black cloth and placed away.

TOOLS OF THE WORK

The ritual blade is needed in most of the rites and you can either use the blade you normally employ in your workings or you may wish to obtain a new one and consecrate it specifically for this Work. This can be a dagger, a sword or any sort of a knife. However, it has to be sharp enough to cut the flesh and to draw blood needed for the rites. For this reason, a simple hunting knife would make a better ritual tool than a fancy athame, which is usually designed solely for decorative, not practical, purposes. You may also use a razor or a needle for ritual bloodletting, but this is all a matter of personal choice. Remember, however, that a blade used to spill blood and to take life is a far better medium to draw the energies from behind the Gates of the Night than a decorative dagger, no matter how fancy and beautiful it is.

In all rituals, you will need seals of spirits and gods. Sometimes they only serve as a focal point for directing the energy. In other workings, they have to be burnt. You should always use the primary sigils of the demon-gods, but the additional sigils and glyphs may work as gateways to their power, as well. The manner of preparation is left to individual choice. For practical reasons, those seals, which are burnt at the height of the ritual, can be simple drawings in black ink on white paper. Black and white sigils are also good for meditative purposes. However, if you prefer to work with the seals in a more fancy form, it is recommended to use only black, red and golden colors. Golden seals on black background or black glyphs on red parchment will work best in these rites. You can also paint them on wood if you prefer a more solid material than paper, but this is not necessary. Finally, all seals and sigils can also be drawn with blood or with an ink mixed with the vital-substance, but then again, it is better to use blood in the ritual itself, to trace the lines of a sigil prepared prior to the working.

All rituals described in this grimoire also require incense, candles and a container to hold the charcoal and to burn the parchments with the sigils. It is recommended to use natural resin incense, burnt on charcoal, or herbal blends which give a great deal of smoke. Thick smoke is an excellent medium for the spirits to manifest and to form into visible shape. Dragon's Blood is specifically associated with Draconian magic but other types of incense with a strong, intense scent will serve purpose as well. Candles should be either red or black, or both. Light as many as you need to conduct the ceremony. It should be bright enough to see the seals and to read the incantations, unless you choose to replace them by your own spontaneous words, and then you will only need a symbolic source of light. The chamber of operation should also be decorated in black and red, with as few other colors as possible.

A specific tool used in the rites of evocation is the mirror. It serves as a living portal to the Other Side, a gateway through which energies of the Nightside flow into the Temple and through which your intent is carried onto the higher planes. The mirror represents the Gates of the Night on the physical plane. It can be opened and activated by the Key of the Night and it can be a powerful vessel for the spirits to manifest in visible form. Mirrors specifically recommended for this Work are simple black mirrors, with smooth, non-reflective surface, large enough to comfortably focus on them in the ritual. The size and the shape of the scrying mirror is always a matter of individual preferences and so it is left to practitioners' choice. In case of a few spirits from this grimoire, however, you will need a black watery mirror. A simple black vessel filled with any black liquid, ink, water dyed black, etc. will be fine for the Work. It should also be large enough to provide a suitable gateway and a point of focus, and it should be consecrated specifically for this Work and not used for any other purpose. All Children of Tiamat are connected with her black ocean and can be called through watery vessels, but some of them prefer the medium of water above other substances of manifestation. It is specified in descriptions of particular spirits whether they should be called into a simple black mirror or through a watery surface. It is strongly advised to read these descriptions carefully before starting preparations for the ritual.

THE OPENING RITUAL

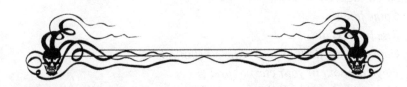

 f you are an advanced practitioner, you may choose to skip the verbal invocation and simply focus on Draconian energies rising within, or you can replace the incantations provided in this grimoire with your personal words, flowing spontaneously from your inner mind in the course of the ritual. But, if you do not feel comfortable with this idea, it is better to use the exact incantations as they are presented here.

INVOCATION OF THE DRAGON

I invoke the Dragon,
Great Monster of Primal Waters!
The First Mother and the Source of All Creation and Destruction!
Monster in the Sea!
Dragon of the Earth!
Great Fiery Serpent who comes with thunder and lightning!
Whose breath is the harsh wind of the desert,
And the nourishing breeze of fresh waters!
Dragon of the Void,
Who swallows the sun at the end of the day!
Dragon of Dark Waters,
Who stirs the ocean of dreams,
And enflames the Desire to seek the Truth!
Great Dragon of the Apocalypse!

I call you by the names:

Tiamat! Leviathan! Lotan! Tannin! Yam! Nahar!
Rahab! Behemoth! Tehom! Hubur! Theli!

Seven-Headed Serpent!
Come forth!
Rise from Within!
Consume my flesh in your timeless flames!
Forge my soul in your eternal fire!
I open the Gates of the Night,
And descend into the Womb of Chaos,
To arise reborn in the Blood of the Dragon,
My body is the Flesh of the Dragon
My blood is the Dragon's vital-essence
My soul is the Flame of the Dragon,
Forever burning in the Darkness of the Night!
And I proclaim my Will through all worlds and all dimensions!

In Nomine Draconis,
Ho Ophis Ho Archaios,
Ho Drakon Ho Megas!

Open your consciousness for the flow of energies and focus on Dragon's force rising within, from the base of the spine, up through the spinal column, into your third eye which opens and suddenly, all illusions are shattered, burnt by the Dragon's Fire. Envision your aura assuming the shape of a fiery dragon. See the wings growing from your back. Feel the energy pressing upon the crown of your head and flowing up. Visualize how the Dragon's Fire rises within and without. You *are* the Dragon, the living manifestation of the primal timeless Current. This is a powerful and ecstatic feeling.

With this assumption of the Dragon form, you can enter any ritual or operation described on the pages of this grimoire.

Invocation of Tiamat

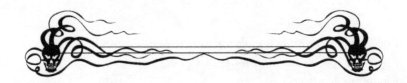

Prepare black candles, a chalice with red wine and a ritual blade. Light the candles, then trace the lines of the sigil with your own blood, visualizing how your vital substance activates the seal and makes it come alive. Put a drop of blood on your third eye, as well.

Concentrate for a while on the sigil while chanting the mantra, *"Ummu Tiamat, Ummu Hubur."*

When the atmosphere in the Temple thickens, draw the Key of the Night with the ritual blade in front of you, and recite the words of invocation:

Ho Ophis Ho Archaios,
Ho Drakon Ho Megas!
Mother of Darkness,
Queen of demons and abominations of the earth,
You hold the Universe in your coiled embrace,
Yours are the keys to the Kingdom of the Night,
Your timeless essence is the soul of the world,
Your blood is the vital force of every living being,
You swallow the Light and cover the world with the Veil of the Night,
In your womb the Black Flame is born,
The fire of creation and destruction,
Which is more ancient than Time.
Ancient Dragon Goddess,
Rise up from the Void!

Vibrate the word, *VOVIN* eleven times.

Envision black shadows in the shape of flames rising from the ground and dancing around you, filling the Temple with intoxicating vapors which wrap around you and penetrate your body, merging into one with your flesh and soul.

When you feel ready to continue the ritual, speak the second part of the invocation:

Come to me, Tiamat!
I offer my flesh as the Temple for your Primal Essence!
I offer my soul as the altar for your Infinite Power!
Mother of Monsters,
Cloak me in your Wings of Shadow,
Fill this ritual space with your Black Fire,
Empower me through your blood,
Lift my soul on your flaming breath,
And let me rise up to the stars.
Open the Gates of the Night for me,
So that I could meet you in the heart of the Void,
Where each thought, desire, and wish become eternal.
Grant me the power to destroy and create,
To burn worlds with your fiery breath,
And to shape them anew from your flesh and blood.
Mother of all souls,
Grant me the keys to your Kingdom of Black Waters,
Open the eyes of my soul so that I could see through illusions,
Awaken my Lust for knowledge and power,
Arouse the Desire of Divinity,
And let your Black Flames consume me from within,
And forever burn in the abyss of my heart,
For Illumination is not found in Light but in Darkness.

Envision yourself surrounded by an enormous pitch black ocean. The waters are quiet at first, but as your invocation rises through the planes, they stir and rise, as well. You can hear waves crushing against an invisible shore and the air in the Temple is being filled with electricity.

Mother of Gods!
I seek your energy, your life, your limitless essence!
I call you forth to enter my being!
In the Abyss of Chaos I claim your heritage of blood!
In Darkness I seek to rest in your eternal arms!

Tiamat! Awaken and rise!
I drink your immortal blood and I offer my own in return!

At this point, you should make an offering of your own blood to the Goddess. Let it drop on the sigil and then, burn the parchment and let the invocation arise through the Gates of the Night into the Void. Drink the wine from the chalice, feeling at the same time that you are being filled up with the dissolving essence of Tiamat. The Black Flame is consuming you from within and you are being transformed through the Dragon's blood in order to rise reborn and empowered.

Focus on this feeling for a while and finish the invocation with the words:

I am the wanderer on the Path of the Ancients,
When I walk, I tread upon the body of the Dragon,
When I sleep, I rest in Dragon's arms,
When my soul flies, it rises on the Dragon's seething breath,
My body is the flesh of the Dragon,
My blood is the liquid fire from Dragon's jaws,
My soul was born in the womb of the Dragon.
I pierce the Veil of the Night with Dragon's Eyes,
And I gaze into Eternity,
Where my Will exists alone.
To see is to know,
To experience is to understand.
To die and re-awaken is to become Divine.
I am the Black Flame that burns in the core of every heart,
I deliver and I devour,
I am the Temple and the Altar,
I am the Dragon,
I am Tiamat.

Envision yourself being drowned and dissolved in the black waters of Tiamat. Feel the connection with the Goddess and let your soul be released from the body as the Draconian force rises and consumes you from within. Let the vision flow freely until the communion is finished. You can also enter the trance of possession through the meditation provided below.

MEDITATION

Sit or lie down comfortably. Envision the black ocean again. You can hear the roar of water and the sound of waves rising and crashing. Suddenly, the water starts pouring into the Temple from all around. It is black and thick. You are being drowned; you cannot move and you cannot breathe. You suffocate and when the water covers everything, all becomes black. Thoughts, emotions, feelings, etc. are shattered and your mind is perfectly empty. The water is warm and it is a pleasant sensation, like being in a womb, immersed in safe and nurturing substance.

Suddenly, you are lifted and you realize that you are hovering above the waters. They are still now. You are no longer in your physical body and you exist as pure consciousness. The ocean is not flat; it is everywhere around, surrounding the whole universe like a cocoon. And in the center, there is Void, Nothingness. Here, you can create things by the power of your Will alone. And you can also destroy your creations. You are one with the Primal Dragon Consciousness, which is limitless and eternal.

Explore this experience – how it feels to look through the eyes of the Dragon, what it is like to be the Dragon.

When the communion of energies is finished, return to your normal consciousness.

SIGIL OF TIAMAT

Mušmahhu

DESCRIPTION, ORIGIN AND MAGICAL POWERS

Mušmahhu belongs to the serpent group of Tiamat's monsters. In historical sources, this entity is most often depicted as a seven-headed snake or dragon and identified with the constellation of Hydra. For this reason, Mušmahhu is also associated with the god, Ningishzida, one of the titles of whom was "The Great Serpent-Dragon" and who was frequently depicted as a horned, winged serpent-dragon, walking on all four legs.

Within works of magic, Mušmahhu assumes several forms, all displaying characteristic features of the spirit's ophidian nature. The demon appears as a blind, horned serpent, holding the eye in its jaws, or as one-eyed serpent with the eye in the center of the forehead or as a snake with a skull and spiral horns instead of the head. The eye burns or glows red or yellow and is connected with the powers of the third eye and the inner vision. Sometimes, the eye looks like a diamond and is shaped like a jewel. The diamond may shine with the fiery energy of the spirit but in its essence it is black, reflecting the absolute blackness of the Void where the demon was born in the Womb of Tiamat. In a similar way, the practitioner invoking Mušmahhu may have visions of glyphs of an eye shaped like a diamond. It is the All-Seeing Eye that was born in the Void from primal sparks of creation. Communion with the spirit is often accompanied by pulsating sensation in the third eye which expands and transcends sensory boundaries of perception.

Mušmahhu is an entity of feminine nature and in rites of evocation she often appears in woman's form with the lower part of the body in the shape of a snake. She holds the power of astral poisoning; her venom might be deadly, but it can also be used for magical protection and immunity. When invoked, she enters the mind and endows the practitioner with the skill of astral shape-shifting. At one time, the practitioner might become a snake, rising up to the heights of the cosmic space. At the other, he might become a spider climbing the Tree of Knowledge and in another, a butterfly drinking the juices from the blooming flowers of the Tree. The astral form of the practitioner becomes fiery and so is the spirit's energy. The concept of the tree or garden is recurrent in the visions obtained during the work with Mušmahhu, as well as dark portals or tunnels in the earth which seem to be gateways into the astral worlds where the practitioner can meet the serpent-goddess. She resides in wild landscapes, forgotten forests and hidden caves. Her hissing voice guides the practitioner through black woods to abandoned ritual places. Her jaws are the caverns of the earth, her teeth are the sharp rocks and her gullet is the underground tunnel. Hence, the possible correspondence on the Tree of Night would be the Lilith qlipha, the lowest qlipothic level, which functions as the gate and portal to the Other Side.

In rituals of evocation, her arrival is heralded by the sigil which appears in the air, glowing with fire or dripping blood. The Temple is filled with clouds of smoke which form into the shape of serpents or a seven-headed hydra. She opens her jaws and reveals the eye which shines like a torch. She incites dreams about shape-shifting, flying and gliding through dimensions in an astral form of a snake. When invoked, she coils around practitioners and devours them in ecstasy of inner illumination, taking them beyond boundaries of flesh. Her mystery is the art of seeing with the Inner Eyes. Her blindness represents limitations of bodily senses. She ignites the primordial spark which rests in the third eye of the practitioner, awakening those senses which exist beyond the veil of human perception.

The Eye of the Blind Serpent

Evocation

Trace the lines of the sigil with your blood chanting the name of the demon. Then, place a few drops of blood on the ritual blade and use it to draw the Key of the Night in the air above the mirror. Focus for a while on how the Key starts to shine and draws the energies of the Other Side into the Temple. Make the offering of life energies or your sexual fluids, sending the intent of the rite through the planes. When this is done, speak the words of evocation:

I call you, Blind Serpent who needs no eyes to see,
I call you, Seven Headed Dragon,
I summon you, Mušmahhu, to manifest in this Temple!
Rise from the bowels of the earth,
Awaken from your sleep in dark caves and forgotten forests!
Come with the poisonous vapors from your jaws,
And illuminate this temple with the fire of your ever-burning gaze!
I open the Gates of the Night,
To call you forth, Mighty Serpent of Primordial Void!
Arise dark and powerful, cloaked in flame, breathing fire,
Hissing arcane secrets in the language of the Ancients,
With Seven Serpents from the Stars,
And with abominations of the earth.
I, ... (your magical name), call you, Mušmahhu, to come and
manifest!
Come to me and assist me in my Work,
Grant me the fulfillment of my Desire which I seek to accomplish,
Which is .... (state the intent of the rite).
Let my Will be done!
I call you by the Key of the Night which opens the Gates and removes

boundaries between the worlds,
I call you by the power of my blood which is the essence of the
Dragon,
And I call you in the name of the Dragon,
In Nomine Tiamat
Ho Ophis Ho Archaios
Ho Drakon Ho Megas!

Now, gaze into the mirror while chanting the name of the demon. Visualize the sigil glowing and dripping blood and see how the mirror becomes a living portal to the Other Side. When you see the shape crystallizing in the black gateway, communicate with the entity. Your intent is already known to the demon and she may grant you what you wish for or you may receive specific instructions on how to proceed further with this operation. When communication is finished, thank the demon and close the working with the words:

In the name of the Dragon,
This is my Will and so it shall be!

Mušmahhu, at first, comes as a swirling vortex of energy, shifting into a mass of snakes or snake heads. Vapors of green phosphorous mist cloak the practitioner in poisonous cocoon which is dense and suffocating. In a more tangible form, you can see her as a blind serpent, in brown and green colors, shifting into half-woman, half-snake. She also appears as a naked woman with a snake coiled around her body. She has dark skin, heavy eye make-up and straight hair in Egyptian manner. She coils around the practitioner, activating the third eye and teaching the art of astral seeing. In works of malediction, she spits the venom into the third eye of the victim, blinding the person and causing scorching pain which spreads from the head onto the whole body in burning agony.

INVOCATION

Place a few drops of your own blood on the sigil of the demon or use the blood to trace the lines of the glyph. With a blooded ritual blade, trace the Key of the Night in front of you, above the altar, and envision it shining and empowering the Temple with fiery Draconian energy. Gaze for a while into the sigil of the spirit, chanting the name of the demon and feel how the lines of the glyph become alive and glow with the energy of Mušmahhu. When the atmosphere in the Temple is charged and you feel ready to begin the invocation, recite the words:

By the Blood of the Dragon which is my own Essence,
And by the Key of the Night,
I call you, Mušmahhu!
Blind Serpent!
Seven Headed Hydra!
Awaken from your sleep in the Womb of Primal Chaos!
Come in tongues of flame and embrace me in your deadly coils,
Fanged and scaled,
Slithering upon my flesh,
And penetrating my soul from within.
Awaken my eyes so that I could see through veils and illusions!
Arise to me from black pits of the earth,
From the dwelling place of serpents, scorpions and worms.
Hear my call and come to me!
Grant me the power to poison the minds and the bodies of my
enemies!
Spit the venom upon their eyes so that they may not see me,
Feed on their souls,
And leave them screaming in burning agony!
Come to me, Mušmahhu!
I offer my body as a vessel for your Ophidian Essence.
Enter this Temple of Flesh,
Enflame my Soul with your primal hunger,
And intoxicate my dreams with visions of power and splendor!
I call you in the name of the Dragon!
In Nomine Draconis!
Ho Drakon Ho Megas!

Burn the parchment with the sigil and let the smoke arise through the planes and carry your wish to be united with the demon. Then, offer yourself to be emblazed with the essence of the spirit. This could be done in sexual ecstasy or by means of visual meditation through which you will enter the trance of possession and let Mušmahhu take over your senses. Enflame yourself to the point in which your soul will cross the boundary of flesh and arise empowered by the very essence of the demon. At this moment, you may let the vision flow freely, enjoying the communion and allowing the spirit to teach you how to use her powers. You may also focus the energy of the demon, which is now yours to command, upon a specific target, especially if you wish to use this power for works of malediction. Envision yourself in the demon form and let your consciousness merge with her essence. Then, envision your victim and, in your snake form, spit the venom in their eyes in order to blind them. Bite the victim in the neck, drawing their blood and life-force, and enjoy this ecstatic and energizing feeling. When you wish to end the working, return to your mundane consciousness, thank the spirit and close the rite.

MEDITATION: SERPENT'S CAVE

Sit or lie in a comfortable position and envision a dark forest on the verge of the night. You are standing on a narrow path leading somewhere deep into the woods. From the distance, you can hear the hissing of a serpent, inviting you to come closer and guiding you through the dark forest paths. While walking, you notice that the hissing becomes louder and clearer and changes into a voice which you can understand in a mysterious way. It speaks to you and guides you further. After a while, the forest ends and you face a huge serpent with spiral horns resembling the horns of a ram. The serpent is blind, her eyeholes are empty and one fiery eye burns in the centre of her forehead. Welcome her with the words, "Ho Drakon Ho Megas." At this moment, the serpent will transform and become a part of the landscape. Her huge jaws are now the entrance to the cave. When you step inside, the entrance closes behind you, like the mouth of a beast, and you feel as if you were in a gullet of a snake. In front of you, there is a long tunnel at the end of which you can see fiery light. While walking through the tunnel, you notice many snakes writhing on the ground and the air is getting more and more electrified. With each step, the tunnel becomes narrower and smaller and soon, you have to crawl to fit in. At the same time, it becomes alive and you are changing, too. Your human limbs disappear and you shape-shift into a serpent, slithering down into another dimension. When you finally reach the end of the tunnel and crawl onto the other side in your serpent form, you find yourself in a completely new place. Look around and explore the landscape. Let the vision flow freely. When you wish to end the vision, return to your normal consciousness.

DREAM WORK: CITY OF THE DEAD

Before going to sleep, gaze into the sigil of Mušmahhu while chanting the name of the spirit. You can use the primary sigil or the seal of the City of the Dead. When you feel the presence of the demon, trace The Key of the Night in front of you and speak the words of dream invocation:

In the name of Tiamat,
I stir the Black Waters of the Abyss,
And I lift the Veil of the Night
To gaze into mysteries which lie beyond the world of Waking.
In the name of the Mother,
I call Mušmahhu to be my guide and companion through dreams
and nightmares.
By the Key of the Night I open the Gateways to Dreamlands,
And I seek to rest in the Arms of the Dragon,
In a dream which will take me to forlorn lands beyond Time,
To the City of the Dead where I shall meet my dark fantasies.
So it shall be!

Then, place the sigil below the pillow. Lie down on the bed and visualize a door with the symbol of the spirit. The symbol starts to glow and the door opens for you to walk through. Focus for a while on visualization given below and then, let yourself fall asleep with the mind focused on the intent of continuing the vision in a dream.

When you walk through the door, you find yourself in the street of a very old city. It looks like a scenery from a few centuries ago. The houses are old and neglected, walls are covered with moss, bricks are scattered all around and the air is thick with the stench of rot. The streets are empty. At the first moment, you cannot see anyone around, then you notice someone in the distance, one person, another, and so on. They walk very slowly, like zombies. The atmosphere of decay is all around and you feel as if you were walking through a strange cemetery. There are bones and skulls of humans and animals lying in the streets. You walk towards a large building that stands out of the other houses. It looks like a huge graveyard mausoleum. There is a symbol on the door, the sigil of Mušmahhu. By the sides of the door, there are guards who look like skeletons dressed in long, dark-hooded robes. Undress yourself and hand them your clothing then, when you are completely naked, enter the temple. Let the vision flow freely while you are falling asleep and explore the place in your dream.

THE CITY OF THE DEAD SIGIL

DRACONIAN SIGIL OF MUŠMAHHU

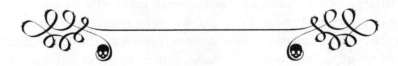

Mušuššu

Description, Origin and Magical Powers

In historical sources, Mušuššu is called the "Furious Snake" and depicted sometimes as a composite creature made up from the parts of a serpent, a lion and a bird. It was associated with various gods and mythological characters, first with Ninazu and Tišpak, then with Ningishzida. It is also often identified as the symbolic animal of Marduk. It has not been connected with any astrological constellation, though. Its early depictions show the creature as a dragon with a lion's head and without talons. Later, the lion parts would be progressively replaced by snake parts. In mythology, Mušuššu originally served the god Ninazu, the king of snakes, and was perhaps a sort of a death messenger, killing with its venom. It is often referred to as "fearless killer" and a very deadly entity.

Within the rites of magic, Mušuššu appears to the practitioner as a vampiric entity manifesting in female human form, connected with necromancy and death principle, feeding on blood and sexual energies. She usually comes as a black bat-like dragon or a winged serpent. She endows the practitioner with the ability to transform the astral body of shadow and to fly through the astral plane as a wraith, a winged vampiric entity who can suck the life-force of a sleeping person. These characteristics resemble the nature of a succubus or an incubus, vampiric demons residing on the dark side of the moon, the qlipothic sphere of Gamaliel, hence, the possible connection to this qlipha. In dreams and visions, she sometimes appears accompanied by creatures of the Sabbat, devils, horned demons, and creatures of the night, inspiring images of orgiastic celebrations and bloody sacrifices. An essential offering to Mušuššu are sexual fluids and blood – substances rich with personal life-force.

Mušuššu comes with wraiths and black shadows emerging from the mirror, casting flickering reflections upon the wall. She is the Black Serpent, arising from winding labyrinths of caves and tunnels beneath the earth, but she is also the black-faced bringer of death. Her upper part of the body is shaped like a human, but does not look human. She has black-scaled skin with a pale shade of blue, her mouth drips with blood, her tongue is protruded and her face is distorted by a grimace of hunger. Her teeth are very thin and sharp and shift into fangs when she transforms into a serpent. She is evoked in sexual ecstasy at cemeteries and burial places, among tombstones, in mausoleums and catacombs, where her manifestations are empowered by the essence of death and sex. She presides over the works of necrophilia and incites eroto-necromantic dreams. You can also meet her in a skeletal form of a wraith, dressed in black hooded robe, holding a large black mirror in her ebony fingers. In this form, she holds dominion over the dead and brings the deceased back from the underworld to manifest through the mirror. By writing the name of a dead person on a parchment with your own blood, you can summon any discarnate soul into the mirror, regardless whether they are willing to come or not.

Invocation of Mušuššu is also experienced as a bitter-sweet union of life and death energies, the Eros and the Thanatos. The serpent comes to bite the practitioner, coiling around to awaken and raise the primal ophidian force, which feels erotic and ecstatic. The body is put into comatose trance and the mind is filled with hunger for life-essence of others. Blood seems as sweet as nectar, it is intoxicating and addictive. The spirit can therefore be used in practices of vampirism and necromancy, works of lunar magic, or astral warfare. The symbol of the spirit should be painted or projected on the forehead – it opens the third eye and aids in astral vision. In ecstatic communion with Mušuššu, you can glide through underground tunnels, walk through walls, swim with streams and rivers and travel across time, to any moment past of future. In works of *malefica*, Mušuššu attacks through the heart, feasting on the warm core and drinking the blood while it is still beating. Her powers can be used in rites of personal empowerment, as well as in hostile sorcery.

EVOCATION

The ritual begins with tracing the lines of the sigil with your own blood while chanting the name of the demon in a low whispering voice. When this is done, place a few drops of blood on the ritual blade and draw the Key of the Night in the air above the mirror which serves as a focal point for the force to manifest. Focus on how the Key shines and draws the energies of the Other Side into the Temple. At this moment, you should make the offering of your sexual fluids and send the intent of the rite through the planes. A sacrifice of life energies can also empower the manifestation. When you feel ready to begin the summoning, speak the words of evocation:

I call you, Furious Snake who feeds on the hearts of the weak,
I call you, Nocturnal Wraith who rules the Kingdom of Shadows!
I summon you, Mušuššu, to manifest in this Temple!
Rise from forgotten graveyards and tombs,
from labyrinths of caves and hidden tunnels of the earth!
Come to me from the black sea of the Night,
with the smoke of incense swirling around,
and with shadows writhing on the walls.
And stand before me in your primal ophidian power,
with hypnotic stare in your smoldering eyes!
I open the Gates of the Night,
To call you forth, Death Messenger,
Dark Initiator of death alchemy and sexual sorcery!
Arise on the wings of Shadow,
with mouth dripping blood and primordial hunger,
Come forth for the feast of flesh!
I, ... (your magical name), call you, Mušuššu, to come and manifest!
Come to me and assist me in my Work,
Grant me the fulfillment of my Desire which I seek to accomplish,

Which is .... (state the intent of the rite).
Let my Will be done!
I call you by the Key of the Night which opens the Gates and removes
boundaries between the worlds,
I call you by the power of my blood which is the essence of the
Dragon,
And I call you in the name of the Dragon,
In Nomine Tiamat
Ho Ophis Ho Archaios
Ho Drakon Ho Megas!

Gazing into the mirror, chant the name of the demon. Again, this is to be done in a whispering voice, low and sensual, like hissing. Visualize the sigil forming from the smoke and glowing red. Focus on how the mirror becomes a living portal to the Other Side. The tool specifically associated with the rites of Mušuššu is the black watery mirror. When you see the spirit assuming visible form in the black gateway or manifesting through the smoke above the altar, communicate with the entity. When this is finished, thank the demon and close the working with the words:

In the name of the Dragon,
This is my Will and so it shall be!

Mušuššu comes willingly, but manifests in a rather ephemeral, evanescent form. It is recommended to conjure her through the medium of smoke and the atmosphere in the temple should be thick with incense, mild resin incense burnt upon charcoal works best. In her ophidian form, she appears as a serpent with bat wings, accompanied by wraiths and shadows. Her eyes are hypnotic and she moves in sensuous, mesmerizing rhythm, putting the practitioner into intoxicating trance. She also comes as half-woman, half-snake, manifesting in clouds of smoke, and tongues of black flame, wild and hissing. She is smoky like a wraith, but she also resembles Medusa, with snakes and/or tentacles writhing around her head instead of hair. She can shape-shift into smoke and in this form, she travels through planes and dimensions. Mušuššu endows the practitioner with the hypnotizing stare which is used in works of malediction to paralyze and drain the power of the victim. Her powers are vampiric and she feeds on blood and life energies. In works of malediction, she rips the victim's chest and belly, devours the beating heart and offers the entrails to Tiamat, the Mother. Apart from practitioner's blood and sexual fluids, she may ask for sacrifice of a living being in which the heart of the victim is to be ripped from the chest and left to bleed out into the chalice as an offering of life energies.

INVOCATION

Open the ritual with placing a few drops of your own blood on the sigil of the demon or use the blood to trace the lines of the glyph. With a blooded ritual blade, draw the Key of the Night in front of you, above the altar and visualize how it shapes from clouds of incense smoke and starts to shine with red light, illuminating the Temple with ghastly brilliance. Gaze for a while into the sigil of the spirit, chanting the name of the demon in low, hissing whisper and feel how the glyph becomes alive, activated by the energy of Mušuššu. When the atmosphere in the Temple is charged, speak the words of invocation:

> *By the Blood of the Dragon which is my own Essence,*
> *And by the Key of the Night,*
> *I call you, Mušuššu!*
> *Furious Snake!*
> *Fearless Killer!*
> *Come to me, Nocturnal Wraith, swaying and writhing in ecstasy of senses!*
> *With phantoms and spectres of the Night,*
> *in sensual fury and ghastly splendor.*
> *Coil around me and pierce my soul with your hypnotic stare,*
> *Bite my flesh and drink my blood in primordial communion!*
> *I offer my body to be consumed in black flames,*
> *In order to arise as your living manifestation!*
> *Penetrate my soul with your forked tongue,*
> *And fill my veins with your Ophidian Essence!*
> *Hear my call and come to me!*
> *Awaken my Hunger!*
> *Grant me the power to travel on the wings of the Night!*
> *Let me feast on the flesh of my enemies!*
> *Rip their hearts and devour their souls,*
> *Take away their power and feed on their vital essence,*
> *And leave them breathless and drained!*

Enter this Temple of Flesh,
Enflame my soul with your consuming Shadow,
And intoxicate my dreams with the ecstasy of nocturnal desires!
I invoke you in the name of the Dragon!
In Nomine Draconis!
Ho Drakon Ho Megas!

Let your call arise through the planes when the parchment with the sigil is burnt and offered through the medium of smoke. Then, enter the trance of possession through visual meditation and by means of sexual ecstasy which is the key to direct communion with Mušuššu. Let the ecstasy take you to the gates of exhaustion and when your soul ascends beyond the boundaries of flesh, your consciousness will merge with the essence of the spirit. At this point, you may let the vision flow freely, enjoying the communion and exploring the powers of the demon, which are now your own, or you may focus the energies upon a specific target. Mušuššu is an excellent teacher of astral vampirism and the art of travelling by night in the form of nocturnal beast of prey. Like other serpent-spirits, she holds the keys to the gnosis of shape-shifting and gliding between worlds and dimensions. She is aggressive and bloodthirsty, but also seductive and mesmerizing. Within rites of malediction, she teaches how to kill and removes moral restraints and hesitation to take life or inflict pain. She arouses hunger for blood, life-essence, and incites thoughts of murder, as well as lust and sexual urges. If you wish to use her energy in works of *malefica*, invoke her powers and envision yourself in the form of a black snake coiling around your victim, inducing hypnotizing trance in which the victim is powerless and unable to fight back. Then, rip their chest and devour their heart, drinking the vital force of your enemy. Enflame yourself with joy and ecstasy and feel how the warm life-essence gathers in your solar plexus and spreads onto the whole body. When you wish to end the working, return to your mundane consciousness, thank the spirit and close the rite.

MEDITATION: TEMPLE OF BLACK SERPENT

Envision yourself in a small temple with black walls, black floor and black ceiling. There are sculptures of serpents around, winged and normal, there are also silver paintings of serpent creatures. In the center of the temple, you notice a fountain in the shape of the serpent. When you touch the water with your hands, chanting the name of the spirit, the water starts flowing rapidly and floods the temple. After a short while, the whole temple is filled with water and the statue of the snake from the fountain becomes alive, it turns into a living black serpent. The water is crystal clear and electrified. It is very cold. The serpent coils around you and bites you again and again until there is not a single spot on your body that would not bleed. Your life warmth is leaving you with each bite and finally the serpent bites you in your third eye. You float from your flesh and watch how it crumbles to pieces like a statue made of ice. The serpent is nowhere to be seen and you realize that you are the serpent now. You can glide smoothly between worlds and dimensions. It feels ecstatic and sexual, also very powerful and invigorating. Enjoy this sensation and let the vision flow freely or explore this power and use it in your further work.

DREAM WORK

Provided below are two meditations that will open your inner mind for the essence of Mušuššu and induce dreams inspired by the spirit. Before going to sleep, gaze into the sigil of the demon, chanting the name in hissing whisper. The primary sigil is recommended for both workings. When you feel the presence of the spirit, trace The Key of the Night in front of you and speak the words of dream invocation:

In the name of Tiamat,
I stir the Black Waters of the Abyss,
And I lift the Veil of the Night
To gaze into mysteries which lie beyond the world of Waking.
In the name of the Mother,
I call Mušuššu to be my guide and companion through dreams and nightmares.
By the Key of the Night I open the Gateways to Dreamlands,
And I seek to rest in the Arms of the Dragon,
In a dream which will take me beyond the Veil of Shadow,
To forgotten temples and ritual places,
Where I shall join forbidden rites and face the Darkness within.
So it shall be!

Place the sigil below the pillow. Lie down on the bed and visualize a door with the symbol of the spirit. Envision the symbol glowing and see how the door opens for you to walk through. Focus for a while on either of the following visualizations and let yourself fall asleep with the mind focused on the intent of continuing the vision in a dream.

Sabbatic Necromancy

When you walk through the door, envision yourself in an old cemetery at night. It is a beautiful, gothic graveyard with statues and ornamented tombstones, stone crypts and mausoleums. It seems forgotten and abandoned, though. The buildings and monuments start to crumble, dust and cobwebs cover the stone, and the whole cemetery is cloaked with thick white fog. Suddenly, you can hear singing coming from the distance and you notice a procession of phantoms emerging from the fog. They look like monks in long robes going to a mass, holding candles which glow with a cold spectral light. The procession walks towards a big, black mausoleum. You follow them and enter the building. The mass is conducted by a naked priest wearing a goat mask which covers his face. On his chest, he has a large tattoo of a black winged snake. A naked woman is lying on the altar, as if in a vision of a traditional Black Mass. But all participants are ghosts. At the climax of the ceremony, the priest thrusts the dagger into the victim's chest, fills the chalice with blood and passes the sacrament around. You drink it with the other participants and you can feel how the elixir transforms your consciousness – you are excited and aroused, it feels like being possessed by the spirit. The priest looks at you and invites you to join the communion: all participants disrobe and a ghastly orgy begins. There are only ghosts, skeletons, zombies and rotting corpses. Join them and let the vision flow in a natural way while you're falling asleep.

Black Lake

Visualize yourself in a dark forest, standing on the shore of a small, pitch black lake. It is nighttime and in the sky above you can see the full moon, but it is very dark, as if in an eclipse, or as if you were looking at its dark side which does not reflect the light of the sun. Summon the demon by whispering or shouting her name into the darkness of the night. After a while, you will see a creature emerging from the lake. She is partially human, but her face is pale and demonic. Her eyes are glowing red and her mouth drips blood. She is dressed in black, windy robes. The demon walks towards you, looking straight into your eyes. Her gaze is piercing and painful and you can feel that your flesh is transforming. You shape-shift into the same creature as the demon. In your mouth, you can sense the taste of blood, which seems to you sweet like the most wonderful nectar and you hunger for more. The demon invites you to follow her and she disappears in the black waters of the lake. You do the same and when you enter the water, you feel that it is not ordinary water but a mirror and a portal to the astral plane. Focus on this feeling while falling asleep and let your instincts and fantasies guide you through visions and dreams.

DRACONIAN SIGIL OF MUŠUŠŠU

Bašmu

Description, Origin and Magical Powers

In Babylonian lore, the word *bašmu* referred to two distinct types of mythological snakes. One of them was called the "Venomous Snake" or *ušum/ bašmu*, which is sometimes interpreted as nothing else than a mythologized form of a natural enemy of man. The other was called the "Birth Goddess Snake" or *muš-šà-tùr/ bašmu* and was a horned type of snake. Bašmu is usually described as a horned snake, either with forelegs or without any limbs. It might be a rearing cobra with horns and in Akkadian, the word *bašmu* was used to denote the Egyptian Uraeus. But, there are also theories that it was a horned serpent with two front legs and wings. Its name is sometimes understood as the "horned serpent with a womb" and it is regarded as an early name for the constellation known later as the Serpent. After Marduk's defeat of Tiamat, Bašmu became one of the symbolic animals of the god Ningishzida, the chthonic deity residing in the Underworld, and was considered a protective entity. Ningishzida is sometimes depicted in human form, with two horned serpents arising from his shoulders. The image of the creature might have been derived from a horned viper called Cerastes, a desert-dwelling animal, which has horn-like protrusions over the eyes.

Within the works of magic, Bašmu usually comes as a flying serpent, brown or golden, with small curved horns and small forelegs, sometimes winged, sometimes without wings, but always soaring high in the air. He rises from lakes, ponds and vessels filled with ink-black water, often manifesting in a ring of fire. He seems to be a mediator between the principles of fire and water. His own essence is fiery, too, and in rites of evocation, he appears with wings of fire, surrounded by flames. A slight stench of sulphur can be scented in the air and tongues of red fire emblaze the Temple with the demon's essence. When the practitioner invokes the spirit into flesh, the astral form changes and flashes with fiery and golden colors and two serpents arise from the shoulders, entwining around the head and expanding consciousness. This perhaps confirms the connection to the Egyptian Uraeus as the crown encircling the head.

Bašmu inspires apocalyptic visions and dreams of earthquakes and disasters, heralding the end of a cosmic cycle, when the whole universe is sucked into a black hole in the centre of the Void, and the beginning of a new aeon, when the world is reborn in the Womb of Chaos. This is the primordial cosmic order: the universe before the birth of life, with the black sun hanging low above the horizon and dripping the nourishing blood over the whole creation. This might perhaps connect the spirit with the Black Sun of Thagirion, the central qlipha on the Tree of Night, but this is a rather loose association. He appears as a fiery serpent and rises up into the cosmic space, devours the sun, the stars and the planets and then, vomits them back in streams of blood, forming a new cosmos in the eternal cycle of renewal.

He endows the practitioner with the ability to use magical fire which is highly venomous and destructive, and teaches how to expand consciousness beyond limitations of flesh. His energy is violent and aggressive and may be used both for protective and destructive purposes. The practitioner can use his essence to empower the flesh by transforming blood into liquid fire and strengthen the aura with impenetrable flames, but the same energy can also be employed in works of malediction to poison the blood of a target and to plague the victim with burning pain. Enflamed with the spirit's essence, the practitioner can shape-shift into a fiery serpent, fly on the wings of flame, breathe fire and burn all that stands in the way.

EVOCATION

Open the ritual with tracing the lines of the sigil with your own blood while chanting the name of the demon. Place a few drops of blood on the ritual blade and draw the Key of the Night in the air above the mirror. It is recommended to use black watery mirror for this working. Focus on how the Key shines and draws the energies of the Other Side into the Temple, and feel the Temple being charged by Draconian fiery essence. At this point, make the offering of life energies or your sexual fluids, sending the intent of the rite through the planes. When you feel ready to begin the conjuration, recite the words of summoning:

I call you, Horned Snake who devours the Sun,
I call you, Venomous Serpent who burns worlds and stars in
apocalyptic fire!
I summon you, Bašmu, to manifest in this Temple!
Arise from black waters of wastelands,
Come forth from primordial Void,
Where the Black Sun sheds deadly rays over the whole Creation!
Come with raging flames,
Clothed with terror,
Scorching and burning all that stands in your way!
I open the Gates of the Night,
To call you forth, Bringer of Apocalypse,
Mighty Serpent of primordial Chaos!
Rise from the heart of the earth,
And stand before me in your fiery ophidian power,
With wings of fire and tongues of flame!
I, ... (your magical name), call you, Bašmu, to come and manifest!
Come to me and assist me in my Work,
Grant me the fulfillment of my Desire which I seek to accomplish,
Which is .... (state the intent of the rite).
Let my Will be done!
I call you by the Key of the Night which opens the Gates and removes
boundaries between the worlds,
I call you by the power of my blood which is the essence of the
Dragon,
And I call you in the name of the Dragon,

In Nomine Tiamat
Ho Ophis Ho Archaios
Ho Drakon Ho Megas!

Focus on the mirror and chant the name of the demon while gazing into the black surface. Visualize the sigil manifesting in the mirror and burning with red flames. Focus on how the black water becomes a living portal to the Other Side. When you notice the spirit forming into visible shape in the mirror gateway, communicate with the entity. When communication is finished, thank the demon and close the ritual with the words:

In the name of the Dragon,
This is my Will and so it shall be!

Bašmu manifests in the Temple with tangible phenomena, the water in the mirror stirs and turns warm, as if heated by fire. Tongues of red flame appear in the mirror and spread all around and finally the spirit shapes into visible manifestation. He may at first appear in his ophidian form, as a black fiery snake with wings of fire. He has small curved horns on his head and thin, sharp teeth. At the conjuror's request, he may also assume a human form, with alien pale skin, big head, large eyes and curved horns. Sometimes, he has a horned skull instead of a head and looks very ghastly, like a phantom. Bašmu holds dominion over venomous fire that burns the world of matter and annihilates boundaries and limitations of flesh. Within rites of malediction, his energies may be used both for personal protection and for magical attack. His venomous essence is an excellent tool for empowering ritual objects employed in death magic: daggers, pins, blades, or razors, which are used to stab or cut the victim, may be saturated with Bašmu's poisonous fire in order to inflict more pain. Sympathetic objects such as puppets or photographs may be burnt in ritual fire empowered by the demon's energies through the rites of evocation. Finally, the spirit's fiery energy can also be channeled and simply directed towards the target. He poisons and burns the victim with his venomous flames, causing agonizing pain.

INVOCATION

Trace the lines of the sigil of the demon with your own blood or simply place a few drops on the parchment. With a blooded ritual blade, draw the Key of the Night in front of you, above the altar, and visualize how it shines with fiery red light, surrounded by red tongues of fire. Gaze for a while into the sigil, chanting the name of the demon and envision how the glyph becomes alive and glows with the energy of Bašmu. When the atmosphere in the Temple is charged and you feel ready to begin the ritual, speak the words of invocation:

By the Blood of the Dragon which is my own Essence,
And by the Key of the Night,
I call you, Bašmu!
Fiery Serpent!
Bringer of Apocalypse!
Come with your venomous flames,
And burn the world so that it could be reborn in the Womb of
Chaos!
Arise with primal terror and fearsome splendor,
And swallow the sun!
Show me how to destroy and create,
How to vomit worlds and devour my enemies!
Hear my call and come to me!
Enter my body which I offer you as Temple,
Cleanse my flesh with your venomous fire,
And lift my soul on your seething breath!
Come from beyond Time,
And teach me how to rise above the stars!
Rain down fire upon my enemies,
And poison the blood in their veins!
Leave them screaming in burning agony!
Enter this Temple of Flesh,
Emblaze my soul with your consuming Fire,
And intoxicate my dreams with the visions of the Black Sun!
I invoke you in the name of the Dragon!
In Nomine Draconis!
Ho Drakon Ho Megas!

Burn the parchment with the sigil and let the smoke carry your call through the planes. Then, let your consciousness merge with the essence of the spirit in ecstatic communion in which the mind will separate from the body and arise on the fiery wings of Bašmu. Use the visual meditation below or enter the trance of possession through sexual ecstasy. Feel how the fiery serpent ascends and coils around your spine and how your soul rises to the stars empowered by his essence. Enflame yourself in the ecstasy when you become the living manifestation of the spirit. Then, let the vision flow freely, enjoying the communion with the demon and exploring his powers, which are now your own, or channel the energies towards a specific target. Envision yourself in the form of the fiery snake and bite your victim, draining their life-essence and poisoning their blood. You can also gather a few drops of venom from the serpent's fangs and let them drip into the third eye of the victim. This causes painful burning sensation in the head which spreads onto the whole body, turning the blood to liquid fire and scorching the flesh from within. When you wish to end the working, return to your mundane consciousness, thank the spirit and close the ritual.

MEDITATION: COSMIC SERPENT

Envision yourself high in cosmic space, looking down on the earth below. You are watching the apocalyptic transformation; the whole planet is falling apart, catastrophes are destroying cities, one by one, and all is consumed by fire. Suddenly, you notice a gigantic fiery serpent with horns arising from the centre of the earth, flying up to the stars. He opens the jaws and swallows the sun. Darkness falls upon the whole universe. For a moment, you cannot see anything and nothing exists. Shortly after, you begin to notice a red glow emanating from you and you can feel the Serpent energy rising from the bottom of your spine. It rises through the chakras, activating and empowering them. After a while, it flows through your whole body and two fiery serpents arise from your shoulders and entwine around your head. At this point, you feel how your consciousness expands and becomes infinite. You become the Serpent and you can swallow and vomit worlds and galaxies. Yours is the power of creation and destruction. You are the only being that exists in the centre of the Void, the beginning and the end of the world. Let the vision flow freely and float with this ecstatic feeling or use the invoked power in your further work.

DREAM WORK

Both meditations provided below can be used in dream work in order to open your inner mind for the essence of Bašmu and to guide you into dreams inspired by the spirit. The primary sigil of the demon is recommended for both workings. Before going to sleep, gaze into the sigil and chant the demon's name for as long as you need to feel the presence of the spirit. Then, trace The Key of the Night in front of you and recite the words of dream invocation:

> In the name of Tiamat,
> I stir the Black Waters of the Abyss,
> And I lift the Veil of the Night
> To gaze into mysteries which lie beyond the world of Waking.
> In the name of the Mother,
> I call Bašmu to be my guide and companion through dreams and nightmares.
> By the Key of the Night I open the Gateways to Dreamlands,
> And I seek to rest in the Arms of the Dragon,
> In a dream which will take me to worlds beyond the stars,
> To forgotten lands and winding labyrinths of the Underworld.
> So it shall be!

Place the sigil below the pillow and lie down on the bed. Visualize a door with the symbol of the spirit and see how it shines with red fire and burns with tongues of red flame. The door opens and you can walk through. Focus for a moment on either of the following visualizations and, while falling asleep, keep your mind focused on the intent of continuing the vision in a dream.

DREAMWORK

Descent into the Underworld

When you walk through the door, envision yourself in a mountainous area. The sun is setting and disappears behind the horizon, and in front of you, there is a golden gateway to the land of the dead. The sigil of the demon is carved on the door and above the gate you can see ornaments in the shape of horns. The gateway is watched by two guards, one armed with an axe, the other with a club. When you put your hand on the symbol, it starts to glow with red fire. Greet the guards in the name of the demon and ask them to open the gate for you. When this is done, enter the hallway. Whisper or chant the name of the demon and ask him to guide you through the Underworld.

He will appear in one of his serpent/dragon forms, possibly as a golden or fiery serpent with horns. Let him guide you through labyrinths and chambers until you reach a huge underground realm in which the only light are the burning rays of the black sun. Let the vision flow freely when you fall asleep and explore the land in a dream.

Land of Fire and Ice

Visualize a gloomy scenery: a wasteland which looks like remains of human civilization after a huge catastrophe. You can still see fire and thick vapors of black smoke hovering above the ruined landscape. Everything is in red, fiery colors. Bones and skulls lie scattered all around and vultures circle above, in search for prey. Call the demon by chanting his name. He will come in the form of a flying horned serpent and will ask you to ride on his back. When you both rise up to the sky, you can watch the black wasteland below. Rivers of fiery lava flow across the landscape and huge black sun rises over the horizon, shedding blood on the whole scenery. Focus on this image while falling asleep and explore this post-apocalyptic world in your dreams.

DRACONIAN SIGIL OF BAŠMU

Ušumgallu

Description, origin and magical powers

Ušumgallu is another serpent-spirit, though it is often identified with a winged dragon as well. In historical sources, this spirit is sometimes mistaken for Bašmu and its attributes are uncertain. The word *ušumgallu* is a derivative from *ušum* and it literally means "Prime Venomous Snake." Its foremost quality is being a determined killer, killing probably with its venom, and frightening even the gods. Also *ušum (gal)* was used as an epithet for certain gods and kings.

In magical work, Ušumgallu usually appears in the form of a golden dragon or a winged golden serpent. It endows the practitioner with the ability to use golden magical fire: either to purify and protect or to destroy. The fire is attached to the palms of the hands and the practitioner can stretch them through the astral plane and touch the subtle body of a target – in order to purify the person's energy, e.g. for healing, or to use it for destructive purposes – to burn the life-force of a victim. When invoked, the spirit enters the body and mind from within, causing the aura to glow with golden radiance and the astral form assumes the shape of a golden dragon. The practitioner can use a mask of a dragon, painted gold, to attract the spirit into the temple of flesh. Emblazed by the spirit's essence in a trance of possession, the mask grows into flesh and the whole body is transformed into dragon-form, which is a very powerful and tangible manifestation.

Within rites of evocation, the demon appears as a royal cobra, dancing, writhing, and hypnotizing the practitioner with his movement and mesmerizing, red-glowing eyes. He bites the third eye and merges with the personal essence, the core of existence, which feels like a very intense activation of this spiritual center, sometimes accompanied by intense pain and visions of bleeding from the third eye. The cobra may also split into two smaller snakes which enter the flesh of the practitioner through the forehead. One of these snakes is silver, the other golden, which brings into mind associations with the Ida and the Pingala, two aspects of the ophidian energy of Kundalini. This also connects Ušumgallu with the Egyptian Uraeus and with Bašmu, the other serpent god who sometimes manifests as two snakes entwined around the head and expanding consciousness beyond boundaries of perception. In ancient Egypt, the Uraeus was the symbol for the goddess Wadjet, one of the earliest Egyptian deities, who was often depicted as a rearing cobra. Her depiction was incorporated into a headwear, a type of a crown encircling the head, worn by the pharaoh as a symbol of divine authority. The royal cobra with a crown on its head is one of the most frequent manifestations of Ušumgallu. The spirit also inspires visions of ancient temples with ornaments depicting cobras, Egyptian drawings and hieroglyphs on walls and columns, and with golden altars and ritual tools. The image of the cobra, splitting into two serpents and coiling around the head, may also be successfully used in invocation and visual meditations.

EVOCATION

The ritual starts with tracing the lines of the sigil with the practitioner's blood, while the name of the demon is being chanted in low, vibrating voice. When this is done, anoint the ritual blade with a few drops of blood and draw the Key of the Night in the air above the mirror to which you summon the spirit. Focus for a while on how the Key shines with golden light and draws the energies of the Other Side into the Temple, empowering the ritual space. Then, make the offering of life energies or your sexual fluids and send the intent of the rite through the planes. When the atmosphere in the Temple is charged and you feel ready to begin the conjuration, speak the words of summoning:

> *I call you, Golden Serpent who flies on the Wings of the Dragon,*
> *I call you, Prime Venomous Snake!*
> *I summon you, Ušumgallu, to manifest in this Temple!*
> *Arise from forgotten temples in the bowels of the earth,*
> *And from secret ritual places beneath the waters,*
> *Come forth to me with your fearsome radiance!*
> *I call you, Golden Cobra, whose flames heal and destroy!*
> *Arise with your golden fire,*
> *Which burns the flesh and liberates the soul,*
> *In ecstatic ascent into worlds beyond the stars!*
> *I open the Gates of the Night,*
> *To call you forth, Venomous Serpent,*
> *Fearless killer and destroyer of the weak!*
> *Spread your golden Dragon wings,*
> *And stand before me in your luminous essence and radiant splendor!*
> *I, ... (your magical name), call you, Ušumgallu, to come and manifest!*
> *Come to me and assist me in my Work,*
> *Grant me the fulfillment of my Desire which I seek to accomplish,*
> *Which is .... (state the intent of the rite).*
> *Let my Will be done!*
> *I call you by the Key of the Night which opens the Gates and removes boundaries between the worlds,*
> *I call you by the power of my blood which is the essence of the Dragon,*
> *And I call you in the name of the Dragon,*
> *In Nomine Tiamat*
> *Ho Ophis Ho Archaios*
> *Ho Drakon Ho Megas!*

Gaze into the black surface of the mirror and chant the name of the demon. Envision the sigil manifesting in the mirror and shining with tongues of golden fire. A round, black mirror with smooth surface is the most suitable key to the gnosis of the spirit. Visualize how the mirror becomes a window onto the Other Side and when you notice the demon forming into visible shape in the gateway, communicate with the entity. When communication is finished, thank the spirit and close the ritual with the words:

In the name of the Dragon,
This is my Will and so it shall be!

In rites of evocation, Ušumgallu appears in his ophidian and draconian forms, hardly ever manifesting in any anthropomorphic shape. He comes as a golden cobra, with scales of gold and with ornaments in Egyptian manner. He has a jewel at the end of the tail and he wears a golden crown on the head. His dragon-form is more often encountered within the works of invocation. The cobra moves around the practitioner in mesmerizing serpentine rhythm, inducing a hypnotic trance. Ušumgallu strikes fast and his venom is deadly. In works of self-empowerment, it fills the aura of the practitioner with golden radiance which serves as a protective shield against magical attacks and returns baneful energy to the sender. His essence is golden and fiery, but the fire possesses a melting and dissolving nature rather than scorching and burning. He bites the victim in the third eye, distorts the vision and poisons the mind. His venomous energy affects the spiritual body of the target, disrupting the natural flow of life energies and inflicting confusion, sickness, and psychic disorders. His essence merges with the victim's consciousness in a very subtle way and is extremely difficult to recognize or banish.

INVOCATION

Open the ritual with tracing the lines of the demon's sigil with your own blood or simply place a few drops on the parchment. With a blooded ritual blade, draw the Key of the Night in front of you, above the altar, and visualize how it shines with golden fire, illuminating the Temple with golden radiance. Focus for a while on the sigil, chanting the name of the demon in low, vibrating voice. Visualize how the glyph becomes alive and glows with the golden energy of Ušumgallu. When you feel ready to begin the ritual, recite the words of invocation:

By the Blood of the Dragon which is my own Essence,
And by the Key of the Night,
I call you, Ušumgallu!
Prime Venomous Serpent!
Royal Cobra with scales of gold!

Come in tongues of golden fire,
Swaying and writhing,
Entranced in serpentine rhythm,
And let your flames consume me from within!
Dissolve the flesh with your sacred venom and free the soul,
So that I could rise on the wings of the Dragon,
In sacred communion with your fearsome essence!
Hear my call and come to me!
Enter my body which I offer you as Temple,
And grant me protection against those who wish me harm!
Fortify me with your powers,
And fill me with your impenetrable radiance!
Confuse the minds of my enemies,
Take away their health and sanity,
Poison their minds and feast on their souls!
Enter this Temple of Flesh,
Spread your golden wings and lift my soul in ecstasy of senses!
Bring me dreams of knowledge, wisdom and understanding!
I invoke you in the name of the Dragon!
In Nomine Draconis!
Ho Drakon Ho Megas!

Burn the parchment with the sigil and let the smoke carry your call through the planes. Then, enter the trance of possession and offer yourself to be enflamed with the fiery energy of the spirit. Use the visual meditations provided below or let your consciousness merge with the invoked essence through sexual ecstasy. Feel how the golden serpent moves up your spinal column and ascends to the third eye, where it becomes the dragon. His fiery wings spread and your soul is lifted beyond the flesh in ecstatic communion. At this point, let the vision flow freely, exploring the powers of the demon, which are now your own, or focus the energies towards a specific target. In rites of invocation, Ušumgallu manifests from within as a fiery dragon or a winged serpent with golden scales. The subtle body of the practitioner is filled with liquid gold, the aura flashes with golden colors, and golden fire arises from spiritual centers on the palms of the hands. This energy has a soothing and healing quality and can be used for protection and empowerment, but it is also very deadly when used in works of malediction. Like in the rites of Bašmu, the target must be hit through the third eye, either by biting and spitting the venom or by burning the chakra with liquid fire. En-vision yourself with flames on the palms of your hands and burn the eyes of the victim, focusing the flow of destructive energies on the target's third eye or assume the astral form or a cobra or a winged venomous snake and bite the victim, poisoning their aura and inflicting sickness and pain. When you wish to end the working, return to your mundane consciousness, thank the demon, and close the ritual.

MEDITATIONS

Royal Cobra

Envision yourself on the beach by the sea. It is dawning and the sun slow-ly emerges from behind the horizon. You are sitting and meditating, star-ing at the rising sun. Suddenly, its golden light flashes and blinds you for a while. Unable to withstand the light, you close your eyes, and when you open them again, you notice that the surrounding scenery has changed. You are no longer on the beach. Now, you are sitting in a golden temple built in an Egyptian manner. Chant the name of the demon. He will appear as a royal cobra – huge, with a crown on its head and a jewel at the end of its tail. The cobra is dancing and moving closer and closer. Suddenly, it strikes and bites you straight into the third eye. You feel pain and you realize that your perception changes, but the cobra transforms, too. It splits into two snakes and they both enter your body through the third eye. You feel how the snakes entwine around your spine, activating a rapid and very intense surge of energy through your flesh. Finally, they both emerge from your third eye and coil around your head. This feels painful for a moment, but then the pain fades away and your consciousness expands, merging with the essence of the demon. Let the vision flow freely and explore the powers you have awakened in yourself.

The Jade Throne

Envision yourself entering a lake or a pond. The water is green and you can hardly see anything beneath. You swim to the bottom of the lake and notice an entrance to a temple. The temple is green and looks like made of emerald with jade ornaments. In the center, there is a jade throne on which sits a huge cobra with a crown on its head. The crown has a purple jewel. When you come closer, the cobra shifts into human form–a young man, looking slightly androgynous. He asks you to disrobe and lie naked on the ground in posture known in Yoga as "cobra." Your legs and hips need to touch the ground, your palms placed upon the floor and the upper part of the body (from navel to head) raised up like a snake, with spine arched backwards and arms straight. Then, he puts the crown on your head, placing the jewel on the forehead, in the area of the third eye. At this moment, you feel that you are shape-shifting into a cobra, your aura turns golden and the crown disappears and grows into flesh, leaving your third eye open and shining with purple energy. Now, your vision is no longer limited by any boundaries of flesh. Explore this feeling and open yourself to whatever will come.

DREAM WORK

Underwater Temple

Before going to sleep, focus for a while on the sigil of Ušumgallu and chant the name of the spirit in low, vibrating voice. When you sense the presence of the demon, trace the Key of the Night in front of you and speak the words of dream invocation:

> In the name of Tiamat,
> I stir the Black Waters of the Abyss,
> And I lift the Veil of the Night
> To gaze into mysteries which lie beyond the world of Waking.
> In the name of the Mother,
> I call Ušumgallu to be my guide and companion through dreams
> and nightmares.
> By the Key of the Night I open the Gateways to Dreamlands,
> And I seek to rest in the Arms of the Dragon,
> In a dream which will take me to subterranean temples,
> Where I shall join forbidden rites and fearsome ceremonies.
> So it shall be!

Then, place the sigil below the pillow and lie down on the bed. Envision a door with the symbol of the spirit which glows and shines with golden fire. The door opens and you are invited to walk through. Focus for a while on visualization given below and let yourself fall asleep, keeping your mind focused on the intent of continuing the vision in a dream.

When you walk through the door of sleep, visualize yourself standing by another door, the entrance to a golden tower with ornaments in the shape of snakes. When you step into the tower, you suddenly notice that there is no floor, only the empty space inside. You fall down into the pitch black water. The walls are smooth and the tower reminds you of a well. Suddenly, you feel that something pulls you by the legs, deeper and deeper into the water, until you reach the bottom. Shortly after, you emerge by the other side of the water which is now seen as a smooth mirror above your head. You realize that you are in a strange underwater temple and you have been dragged here by priestesses who reside in this place. They partially resemble mermaids, but their faces are not completely human; their skin is ghastly pale with a greenish hue and their eyes are all black. The temple is round with white walls and a small altar in the center. Above the altar, you can see the seal of the demon. On the altar, there is a golden chalice, a dagger and a golden mask of a dragon. Cut your hand and let the blood pour into the chalice. Then, put on the mask, call the demon and drink the sacrament from the chalice. Now, let the vision flow freely and let it shape your dreams while you fall asleep.

DRACONIAN SIGIL OF UŠUMGALLU

LAHAMU

DESCRIPTION, ORIGIN AND MAGICAL POWERS

The monster Lahamu (called also *lahmu* or *lahami*) bears the same name as one of the primeval gods created by Tiamat, but he rather seems to be a distinct entity. His name means "the hairy one" and he is sometimes identified with the Babylonian hero or a protective deity associated with such gods as Enki or Marduk. The word *lahama* was used to denote fifty spirits in service of Enki and later, it referred to guardian statues which stood in the gateways of great temples.

Within the works of magic, Lahamu assumes the form of a fiery demon-warrior with long flaming hair and appears on battlefields or places of bloodshed. Sometimes, he has a staff in the shape of a serpent, casting lightning. On other occasions, his very arms are in the form of lightning bolts. His energy is fiery, violent and extremely aggressive. He comes with rage and fury and he endows the practitioner with knowledge of magical warfare with the use of fire and lightning. In rites of evocation, he is sometimes accompanied by his twin sister who embodies forces opposite to his own powers. While the essence of Lahamu is fire and lust, his female counterpart represents death and entropy. Her energy is cold and she manifests with visions of filth and waste. She is a ruthless vampire who feeds on life-force of her victims and when evoked, she appears in the form of a huge spider with a human head, torso and arms. She has six arms and all of them have blades instead of hands and forearms. She is called to the Temple by the same formula, as her male counterpart and by the same name. Also, both forms may be successfully used in rites of malediction and personal self-empowerment. However, she comes on rare occasions and it is easier and more natural to establish contact with the male, fiery form of Lahamu.

Lahamu, himself, has vampiric qualities, as well. When invoked, he enters consciousness with an intense surge of energy, yet this is often experienced by the practitioner as being devoured and deprived of personal life-force, while the nerves are being filled with fire and electricity, the energy of the spirit. This is an ecstatic and erotic experience. Communion of energies occurs through a particular type of sexual union. He bites his forearm and lets you drink his essence, while he drinks yours. It feels erotic, but the consumption is not through flesh and sexual fluids but through blood, by devouring each other in ecstatic union until your consciousness entirely merges with the essence of the demon. His blood tastes metallic and it is invigorating and rejuvenating. He comes with tongues of flames and lightning, which coil around like snakes and consumes your vital force, replacing it with the fiery energies of the spirit as you lie naked on his altar. A rite of invocation leaves the practitioner empowered and focused, alert and excited, but not actually aroused in sexual way. He is called through the sacrifice of sexual fluids, but energies released through erotic ecstasy are sublimated and channelled into the intent of the work.

He inspires electric, fiery and ecstatic visions and he brings dreams of forgotten shrines located somewhere in the desert, rivers of blood flowing into underground temples, and altars surrounded by rings of fire. Because of violent and destructive aspects, he might be associated with the qlipha Golachab, the dark and fiery counterpart of Geburah, represented by violent spirits of wrath. Yet, because of the spirit's masculine and sexual aspects, he might also belong to the level of Ghagiel, ruled by the Dark God of the Qlipoth who brings apocalypse to the world and destroys the universe.

EVOCATION

Trace the lines of the sigil with your own blood while chanting the name of the demon. When this is done, place a few drops of blood on the ritual blade and draw the Key of the Night in the air above the mirror. Envision the Key glowing with fire and lightning and drawing fiery Draconian energies from the Other Side into the Temple. Make the offering of life energies or your sexual fluids and send the intent of the rite through the planes. When you feel ready to begin the conjuration, recite the summoning:

I call you, Fearsome Warrior who comes with fire and fury,
I call you, Guardian of Forgotten Temples!
I summon you, Lahamu, to manifest in this Temple!
Awaken from your slumber behind the Gate of Sunset,
And come with wrath and lust,
Fire and brimstone!
Arise from the land of no return,
With mysteries more ancient than time!
I open the Gates of the Night,
To call you forth, Fierce Demon Warrior!
Through the river of blood and the ring of fire,
Clothed in wolf skin,
With flaming hair,
And serpents coiling around.
Stand before me in your primal power,
And crush the world in your deadly embrace!
I, ... (your magical name), call you, Lahamu, to come and manifest!
Come to me and assist me in my Work,
Grant me the fulfillment of my Desire which I seek to accomplish,
Which is .... (state the intent of the rite).
Let my Will be done!
I call you by the Key of the Night which opens the Gates and removes
boundaries between the worlds,
I call you by the power of my blood which is the essence of the
Dragon,
And I call you in the name of the Dragon,
In Nomine Tiamat

Ho Ophis Ho Archaios
Ho Drakon Ho Megas!

Now gaze into the mirror and chant the name of the demon. Visualize the sigil manifesting in the mirror, shining with fire and lighting. Envision how the mirror becomes a gateway, a living portal, and focus on the energies flowing through the sigil into the Temple and back to the Other Side. When you notice the demon forming into visible shape in the mirror gateway, communicate with the spirit. When communication is finished, thank the demon and close the working with the words:

In the name of the Dragon,
This is my Will and so it shall be!

In rites of evocation, Lahamu appears as a fiery warrior, fierce and strong, with dark red skin and flaming hair. His teeth are thin and sharp, like the teeth of a beast. His eyes glow amber. Instead of forearms and hands, he has writhing serpents which shift into bolts of lightning. His essence is both fiery and electric, furious and lustful. An offering of sexual fluids is essential, both in rites of evocation and invocation. But, above all, he has to be evoked through blood, both human and animal. In works of hostile sorcery, he strikes the target with lightning, tearing through protective shields, and rips the spiritual body, feasting on vital forces of the victim. The attack triggers a rush of adrenaline into the blood of the target and makes the blood flow faster. This is a form of astral vampirism, a mixture of pain and delight, which leads to a rapid loss of vital energies. At the time of full moon, Lahamu sometimes appears as a dark hunter with face shifting into a skull, clothed with wolf skin and wearing a horned helmet with deer horns. He holds a spear in one hand and a chalice in the other, drinking the blood of slain victims. Both forms can be successfully employed in astral vampirism and other rites of malediction.

INVOCATION

Place a few drops of your own blood on the parchment with the sigil of the demon or use the blood to trace the lines of the glyph. With a blooded ritual blade, trace the Key of the Night in front of you, above the altar and envision it shining with red flames mixed with the bright radiance of lightning. Focus on the sigil, chanting the name of the demon, and see how the lines of the glyph become alive and glow with the fiery energy of the spirit. When the atmosphere in the Temple is charged and you feel ready to begin the invocation, speak the words:

By the Blood of the Dragon which is my own Essence,
And by the Key of the Night,
I call you, Lahamu!
Fiery Warrior,
Fearsome Demon of Lust and Fury!
Come from forgotten temples,
And from blood-dyed battlefields,
Behind the Gate of the Setting Sun!
Come with flaming lashes which burn the earth,
And scourge the souls of the living!
I offer myself on the altar of your sexual sorcery,
And I drink your venomous blood,
My body is a vessel for your living fire!
Arise with tongues of flames and lightning,
Penetrate my soul from within,
Stir my blood with your seething breath,
And fortify my flesh with your fearsome essence!
Grant me the power to weaken and destroy my enemies!
Devour their vital force,
Feast on their tortured souls,
And leave them writhing in burning agony!
Enter this Temple of Flesh,
Intoxicate my Soul with your primal hunger,
And enflame my dreams with terror, lust and ecstasy!
I invoke you in the name of the Dragon!
In Nomine Draconis!
Ho Drakon Ho Megas!

Burn the parchment with the sigil and let the smoke arise through the planes and carry your wish to be united with the spirit's essence. Then, use the visual meditation below to enter the trance of possession, or merge your consciousness with the energies of the demon by means of sexual ecstasy. In rites of Lahamu, both methods are recommended. Feel how the spirit enters your body through the third eye and while his flames ascend and coil around your spine, let your soul be enflamed in communion with this fiery essence. You may now let the vision flow freely and explore the powers of the spirit, which are yours to command, or you may channel the force upon a specific target. Absorption of energies occurs through sexual union, both in works of self-empowerment and in rites of malefic sorcery. Envision yourself in the form of the demon-warrior and focus the energies of rage and fury in your hands which are visualized as fiery bolts of lightning. Strike your target through the third eye and through the throat, making the victim blind and mute, unable to see you or to banish the force. Visualize how the fire and lightning tear through protective layers of the aura, stripping the target of defensive powers, and finally, rip the victim's body in furious rape, consuming their vital force through delirious agony and leaving them exhausted to the verge of death. When you wish to end the working, return to your mundane consciousness, thank the demon, and close the ritual.

Meditation: Fiery Warrior

Envision yourself in a huge battlefield with hundreds of corpses and dying warriors strewn about. The whole scenery looks more ancient than modern, with old weapons and archaic armors. There is a stench of burning and bloodshed in the air. Black clouds hang low above the horizon and the sky is blood-red, as if it had been dyed by the blood spilt on the fields around. The air is slightly electrified and you can feel anxiety, as if the worst was still about to happen. Suddenly, from clouds of smoke, the demon-warrior arises. He is taller and stronger than any human being. His skin is dark red and his long hair is fiery. He has long, writhing serpents instead of forearms and hands. You can sense the aura of savageness and battle-rage surrounding him. He is heading straight for you and he knocks you down. At this moment, his snake-arms change into lightning bolts. He strikes one of them into your third eye, the other into your throat. The pain is tearing you apart and for a while, the whole scenery fades into black. Shortly after, you recover consciousness and you realize that you are no longer lying on the ground. Now, you are standing where the demon stood before. You are him – you have his fiery essence and his snake arms. You see what he sees and you feel what he feels. You can now give in to this feeling and let the vision flow freely. You can also experiment with this fiery essence and focus it on a chosen target.

DREAM WORK: TEMPLE OF FIRE

Before going to sleep, focus for a while on the sigil of Lahamu while chanting the name of the demon. When you sense the presence of the spirit and the air is slightly charged with energies of fire and lightning, trace the Key of the Night in front of you and speak the words of dream invocation:

In the name of Tiamat,
I stir the Black Waters of the Abyss,
And I lift the Veil of the Night
To gaze into mysteries which lie beyond the world of Waking.
In the name of the Mother,
I call Lahamu to be my guide and companion through dreams and
nightmares.
By the Key of the Night I open the Gateways to Dreamlands,
And I seek to rest in the Arms of the Dragon,
In a dream which will take me to forgotten temples in the heart of
the desert,
Where I shall taste the ecstasy of blood and lust,
Through the ancient gnosis of the Demon Warrior.
So it shall be!

Place the sigil below the pillow and lie down on the bed. Close your eyes and envision a door with the symbol of the spirit shining with the mixture of red flames and the bright radiance of lightning. The door opens and you can walk through. Focus on visualization given below and, as you fall asleep, keep your mind focused on the intent of continuing the vision in a dream.

When you walk through the door, visualize yourself in a desert scenery. The sand, the sun and the sky are red. As you walk forward towards the setting sun, you notice a small round shrine on a hill. It has no walls, only columns. Bolts of lightning strike around the shrine, even though there is no storm and the whole atmosphere seems rather dreamy and hypnotic. When you come closer, you realize that the shrine is a part of a larger temple and you are standing by the entrance which leads downstairs, under the ground. By the sides of the door, there are two statues of warriors with long hair, both holding staffs in the shape of snakes. When you go down the stairs, you feel that the air grows hot and dry. Vapors of strong incense intoxicate you and you become even more sleepy. When you enter the main chamber, you notice another statue of a warrior, resembling the ones by the entrance.

He is naked, with a muscular, athletic body. He has fiery hair and his eyes are empty. Apart from the statue, there is only a small altar in the chamber on which you can see an empty chalice and a dagger. Take the blade and make an offering of your own blood, letting it drop into the chalice. When it is full, pour the blood on the statue. It will become alive and turn into the demon-warrior. Speak to him and let him guide you through your dreams.

DRACONIAN SIGIL OF LAHAMU

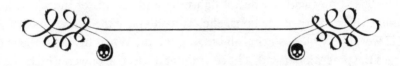

UGALLU

DESCRIPTION, ORIGIN AND MAGICAL POWERS

Ugallu, also known as "The Great Storm" demon in source literature, is referred to as "hurricanes." It is often described as a lion-headed entity associated with the gods of the Underworld such as Nergal. In this sense, the demon is the punisher of transgressors and the bringer of disease. Sometimes, it is depicted with a mace and an upraised dagger and regarded as a protective entity. The name of the spirit translates as the "Big Weather Beast" and it is thought to be the adversary of the Sun God or an associate of the storm god Adad. Violent weather phenomena such as roaring storms were imagined as "released from the sky" and personified by leonine monsters. It is probable that Ugallu is one of these mythological creatures.

Within works of magic, the spirit manifests powers connected with air, electricity and water. Ugallu has feminine nature and in rites of evocation, appears either as an abstract vortex of energy or in anthropomorphic female form, airy, translucent and made up from the essence of shadows and black clouds. She comes with flashes of lightning and sounds of thunder which resemble the roaring of the lions. She claims to have the power to blast the whole world by violent storms and raging winds. When invoked, the spirit charges the practitioner with a huge amount of electric power, which can be used for magical purposes. This feels like a rapid and extremely ecstatic ascent of energy along the spinal column, focused in the third eye. A whirling vortex opens in the centre of the forehead, connecting the mind with the energies of the spirit which manifest through the astral plane. By controlling the astral vortex of chaos, the practitioner can "stir" the force and cause changes on material plane, influence events, inflict damage on the enemy, and shape reality. The essence of this energy is highly destructive and when focused, it is possible to cast this astral force as a powerful lightning bolt in magical combat. If trained, this practice is a very powerful magical weapon.

It is easiest and most natural to establish contact with this spirit through dreams. Ugallu inspires dreams of flying, levitating and travelling through the air, riding on storms and rising on tongues of lightning. In a trance of possession, she lifts the soul beyond the flesh in ecstatic flight over dark waters, unquiet lakes and raging seas. The astral form of the practitioner shifts into a black wraith and flies through the planes on the wings of shadow. On the qlipothic Tree of Night, this demon might perhaps be associated with A'Arab Zaraq, the astral sphere of storms and lightning, connected with water and the energy of Dark Venus.

EVOCATION

Trace the lines of the sigil with a few drops of your own blood while chanting the name of the demon. Then, anoint the ritual blade with blood and draw the Key of the Night in the air above the mirror, which is the focal point for the energies. It is recommended to use the water mirror in this specific working, but an ordinary black mirror will also be suitable. Envision the Key shining with blue electric radiance and drawing the energies of the Other Side into the Temple. At this point, make the offering of life energies or your sexual fluids and send the intent of the rite through the planes. When the atmosphere in the Temple is slightly electrified and you feel ready to begin the ritual, speak the words of conjuration:

I call you, Great Storm Demon who comes with roaring hurricanes,
I call you, Mighty Weather Beast!
I summon you, Ugallu, to manifest in this Temple!
Arise from unquiet waters in the Womb of Chaos,
From black seas and oceans,
Where the primordial terror is born!
Come with thunder and lightning,
Clothed with tremendous gloom,
With harsh winds and savage storms,
Which rip the sky and torture the earth!
I open the Gates of the Night,
To call you forth, Fearsome Hurricane!
Stir the clouds and raise the waters,
And stand before me in your fierce power,
In splendor and fury,
Roaring across the worlds and dimensions!
I, ... (your magical name), call you, Ugallu, to come and manifest!
Come to me and assist me in my Work,
Grant me the fulfillment of my Desire which I seek to accomplish,
Which is .... (state the intent of the rite).
Let my Will be done!
I call you by the Key of the Night which opens the Gates and removes
boundaries between the worlds,
I call you by the power of my blood which is the essence of the
Dragon,
And I call you in the name of the Dragon,
In Nomine Tiamat
Ho Ophis Ho Archaios
Ho Drakon Ho Megas!

Gaze into the mirror while chanting the name of the demon. Visualize the sigil manifesting in the mirror and shining with bright electric energy with flickering shades of blue. Envision how the mirror becomes a window onto the Other Side and a gateway for the energies which flow into the Temple. When you notice the shape crystallizing in the black gateway into visible form, communicate with the entity. When communication is finished, thank the demon and close the ritual with the words:

In the name of the Dragon,
This is my Will and so it shall be!

Ugallu's essence is airy and ephemeral. It is also very chaotic and the spirit has to be specifically asked to assume a tangible shape when manifesting in the mirror. In rites of evocation, Ugallu usually appears in human form, as a demonic female, but her face may be shifting from female into male, from young into old. She has white disheveled hair which shifts into bolts of lightning and her face is distorted with a manic look of madness. In her hands, she holds a staff made of bones and skulls, the emblem of her powers, with which she commands the winds and stirs the clouds. She also comes as a dark figure with arms crossed, dressed in a black robe, with the face hidden under the hood. When she lifts the hood, you can see a whirling vortex in the centre of her forehead. Ugallu enters the body of the victim through the third eye and rips the aura with the essence of lightning. Her energy is electric and when focused on a target, it feels like being struck by lightning or electrocuted. It spreads throughout the body in agonizing waves, which may result in variety of physical damage, especially circulatory and cardiac disorders. In rites of malediction, she ensures a violent and painful death.

INVOCATION

Open the ritual with placing a few drops of your own blood upon the sigil of the demon or use the blood to trace the lines of the glyph. With a blooded ritual blade, draw the Key of the Night in front of you, above the altar, and visualize how it shines with blue flickering radiance, charging the Temple with electric energy of the spirit. Gaze for a while into the sigil, chanting the name of the demon, and visualize how the glyph becomes alive, activated by the essence of Ugallu. When you feel ready to begin the ritual, speak the words of invocation:

By the Blood of the Dragon which is my own Essence,
And by the Key of the Night,
I call you, Ugallu!
Fearsome Demon of lightning and thunder!
Roaring Hurricane!
Come with dark clouds and blacken the sun!
Awaken the winds and raise the waters!

Arise from the heart of the Void,
With delirious fury that none can withstand!
Come with the roaring of the lions,
With storms raging across the oceans,
And wreaking havoc on the land!
Enter this body which I offer you as Temple,
And free my soul through your rites of torture and ecstasy!
Hear my call and come to me!
Grant me the power to command storms and lightning,
To rule the Vortex of Chaos,
And to create and destroy!
Crush my enemies and feast on their flesh,
Cloak their souls in consuming darkness,
And plague them with death, famine and strife!
Enter this Temple of Flesh,
And lift my Soul on tongues of lightning!
Let it rise on your fearsome breath,
And bring me dreams of terror and fury!
I invoke you in the name of the Dragon!
In Nomine Draconis!
Ho Drakon Ho Megas!

Burn the parchment with the sigil and let the smoke arise through the planes with your wish to be united with the demon. Then, enter the trance of possession through visual meditation or through sexual ecstasy, and let your consciousness merge with the energy of the spirit. Feel how the essence of the demon enters your flesh through the third eye and spreads onto your whole body in waves of electricity. This may feel at first painful but then your soul will be lifted beyond the flesh in ecstatic communion. You may now let the vision flow freely, exploring the powers of the demon which are now yours to command, or you may focus the energies upon a specific target. Ugallu manifests in rites of invocation as a vortex of electric energy arising in the third eye and flowing through the spinal column. This energy is very destructive and the practitioner can use it in magical attack to cast lightning bolts through the astral plane. Envision how it strikes the target in the third eye and rips the subtle body of the victim, tearing through protective shields and weakening defense mechanisms. If you wish to use Ugallu's essence for personal protection and empowerment, invoke the spirit and visualize yourself surrounded by blue flickering chains of electricity which form a defensive shield against magical attacks. When you wish to finish the working, return to your mundane consciousness, thank the spirit, and close the ritual.

MEDITATION: STORM PORTAL

Envision yourself standing on the shore of a sea or ocean. The air is moist and electrified, as if before the storm. From the distance you can hear roaring sounds of thunder and you notice flashes of lightning. It is dark and gloomy, even though this is not nighttime. The sky is hidden behind thick black clouds which hang low above the horizon. You are staring at the sea and you realize that the waves are not ordinary water but waves of energy flowing from one world to another. Imagine that they can take you to the Other Side, into another dimension. Start chanting the name of the demon. At the same time, the storm is getting closer and closer. The sea and the clouds seem to merge into one, and darkness cloaks the whole landscape. Bolts of lightning strike one by one around you and the roar of thunder sounds like the roaring of a lion or a savage beast. Suddenly a bolt of lightning strikes you straight in the forehead. You can feel the surge of electricity flowing from your head and spreading onto your whole body. You rise up to the sky, carried by a powerful electric current, while lightning strikes you again and again, empowering your flesh and your soul. Finally, the energy accumulates in your third eye and for a while you feel pain tearing your head apart, but then you realize that you can see the world around in a completely different way than before. It feels like you were blind and now you can see. Your sight has no limits and electric energy flowing through your body endows you with the power to destroy anything that gets in your way. Let the vision flow freely, shaped by the essence of the spirit and by your own imagination or use the energy for further magical work.

DREAM WORK: VORTEX OF CHAOS

Before going to sleep, focus on the sigil of Ugallu and chant the name of the demon. At the same time, envision how the air is being slightly charged with electricity. When you sense the presence of the spirit, trace the Key of the Night in front of you and speak the words of dream invocation:

> In the name of Tiamat,
> I stir the Black Waters of the Abyss,

And I lift the Veil of the Night
To gaze into mysteries which lie beyond the world of Waking.
In the name of the Mother,
I call Ugallu to be my guide and companion through dreams and
nightmares.
By the Key of the Night I open the Gateways to Dreamlands,
And I seek to rest in the Arms of the Dragon,
In a dream which will take me to forlorn mountain tops,
Above roaring oceans and formless clouds,
Where I will learn to command storms and lightning.
So it shall be!

Place the sigil below the pillow and when you lie down on the bed, envision a door with the symbol of the spirit which shines with blue flickering radiance. The door opens and you can walk through the Gates of Sleep. Focus for a while on visualization given below and let yourself fall asleep, with your mind focused on the intent of continuing the vision in a dream.

When you walk through the door, visualize yourself standing on the top of a high rock. It reaches high above the clouds which cover all that lies beneath. The clouds are dark and the atmosphere is gloomy and stormy. Shout the name of the demon and wait for the answer. You will hear a loud thunder which sounds like the roaring of a lion and the clouds will crystallize into a shape of the entity. The spirit has human form with the face which is neither female nor male, neither young nor old, displaying features of both. White disheveled hair resemble bolts of lightning and there is madness in her/his eyes. S/he is wearing long windy robe and holds a staff with which s/he can stir the clouds and rule the winds. The staff is made of bones, chains and skulls. On the demon's forehead, there is an eye which looks like a swirling vortex. S/he touches you with the staff on your forehead and you feel how a similar vortex is opening in your mind. You are transforming. Your human form disappears and you shape-shift into a creature flying through the air, a wraith or a bird with wings of shadow. Use this form to fly into a sleeping trance and explore the worlds beneath in your dreams.

DRACONIAN SIGIL OF UGALLU

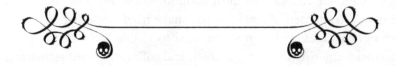

Uridimmu

Description, Origin and Magical Powers

In historical accounts, Uridimmu is described as "raging hounds." It is also known either as the "Mad Dog" or as a human-headed lion-man. In literature, specifically, Babylonian mythology, it is uncertain whether the spirit is a lion or a wolf, as it is also associated with the constellation of the Wolf/Lupus in the southern sky. It is usually depicted as a creature with a human head and torso, set up on lion's hindquarters. It is often paired with the Bull-man (Kusarikku) as an attendant to the Sun God Shamash, and sometimes it is thought to be a protective entity, bringing health to a sick person. The latter is obviously the spirit's new function, attached by the cults of Marduk, but originally Uridimmu was one of the fiends and bringers of evil.

Within works of magic, Uridimmu manifests as the ruler of the Black Desert and the spirit of wastelands devoid of any light. He appears as a vague black shape which has distinctive canine features, sometimes forming from dark clouds, sometimes crystallizing in the middle of the cosmic void. He tears the world apart and endows the practitioner with the ability to see beyond mundane reality. His most common form, however, is that of an alien hybrid composed of tentacles and snake heads shooting out from the vortex of black energy. When summoned to visible form, he manifests as black smoke entering the Temple, thick and suffocating, but sometimes he also appears as a black lion or a wolf, or a mixture of both. When asked, he assumes anthropomorphic shapes suitable for rites of evocation.

Uridimmu inspires visions and dreams of an Everlasting Night in the Black Desert, where he manifests as a part of the living Darkness. It is a barren wasteland, with no living beings and no trace of civilizations, like a landscape after a cosmic catastrophe or before the rise of any life. He also appears in the city of black pyramids, with hundreds of buildings and constructions made of unearthly material, neither metal nor stone. When invoked, he rips the practitioner's flesh and releases the spirit, which is experienced as painful but enlightening. He wraps the body in his black essence, which is dense and stifling, and transforms the soul through his nuclear force. It feels like being devoured by a black cosmic hole which is alive and swallows everything, including worlds, stars, galaxies, and he decomposes all matter into pure energy. He is the Black Wind, which isolates and destroys. His essence is primal undefined energy, which can blast the whole universe. In rites of malediction, he provides the practitioner with a powerful force of destruction, but his atavistic energy requires enormous strength and focus in order to be used successfully.

EVOCATION

Open the ritual by tracing the lines of the sigil with your own blood and chanting the name of the demon. When this is done, anoint the ritual blade with a few drops of blood and draw the Key of the Night in the air above the mirror. Envision the Key glowing with purple fire and drawing Draconian energies from the Other Side into the Temple. At this point, make the offering of life energies or your sexual fluids and send the intent of the rite through the planes. When you feel ready to begin the summoning, recite the words:

> I call you, Fearsome Wolf Demon who comes with the roaring of lions,
> I call you, Black Wind of the Desert!

I summon you, Uridimmu, to manifest in this Temple!
Arise from the Womb of Everlasting Night,
Awaken from your sleep in barren wastelands,
In the Heart of the Empty Space.
Come with forbidden knowledge,
With rites and mysteries more ancient than the stars,
And cloak the world in your consuming darkness!
I open the Gates of the Night,
To call you forth, Bringer of Nothingness!
Destroyer of worlds and galaxies!
Come from beyond Time,
And stand before me with rage and fury,
Clothed with the Essence of the Void,
Fierce and powerful!
Arise with clouds of black smoke,
And blast the universe with your nuclear force!
I, ... (your magical name), call you, Uridimmu, to come and
manifest!
Come to me and assist me in my Work,
Grant me the fulfillment of my Desire which I seek to accomplish,
Which is .... (state the intent of the rite).
Let my Will be done!
I call you by the Key of the Night which opens the Gates and removes
boundaries between the worlds,
I call you by the power of my blood which is the essence of the
Dragon,
And I call you in the name of the Dragon,
In Nomine Tiamat
Ho Ophis Ho Archaios
Ho Drakon Ho Megas!

Gaze into the mirror while chanting the name of the demon. Envision the sigil manifesting in the mirror, shining with dim purple radiance. Visualize how the mirror becomes a gateway to the Other Side, a living portal through which the energies of the spirit are flowing into the Temple from the Black Desert of the Night. When you notice the demon manifesting in the gateway, communicate with the spirit. The essence of Uridimmu is intangible and amorphous and he has to be specifically asked to assume a form suitable for communication. It is also recommended to prepare a sacrifice of a living being, otherwise the demon will drain energy needed for manifestation from the conjuror. When communication is finished, thank the spirit and close the working with the words:

> *In the name of the Dragon,*
> *This is my Will and so it shall be!*

In rites of evocation, Uridimmu manifests first as a cloud of black smoke, a swirling vortex of black energy forming into shapes, or as an amorphous mass of tentacles and snake heads. There are usually seven heads and each of them has only one eye, in the centre of the forehead. Sometimes, the jaws open and other heads emerge from their mouths. These look human, but have no eyes and are completely blind. Their skin is wrinkled, their mouths drip blood and they have thin, sharp teeth. It is hardly possible to communicate with the spirit in this form, and he has to be asked to assume a shape more suitable for communication. Then, he appears in human form, but his skin is dark, his nails are claws and his face resembles a wolf, a savage predator. In works of hostile sorcery, Uridimmu strikes the target through the chest, tearing the flesh and feeding on life energies. The heart is ripped out and devoured, and the body turns black, as if burnt. This can manifest as a disease, which deprives the target of vital forces or as an accident with fire and burning. The victim's soul is torn to pieces and swallowed, while the flesh is left empty and slowly withers until the last spark of life is consumed. This is a slow and agonizing death.

INVOCATION

Place a few drops of blood on the parchment with the sigil or use the blood to trace the lines of the glyph. Then, anoint the ritual blade and trace the Key of the Night in front of you, above the altar. Envision it shining with purple fire, empowering the Temple with the essence of the spirit. When this is done, focus on the sigil, chant the name of the demon, and visualize how the lines of the glyph become alive. A gateway is opened within your inner mind and you are ready to receive the energies of the demon. When the atmosphere in the Temple is charged, recite the words of invocation:

> *By the Blood of the Dragon which is my own Essence,*
> *And by the Key of the Night,*

I call you, Uridimmu!
Fierce Wolf Demon!
Messenger of the Void!
Come from the Desert of Night,
Arise from atavistic depths beyond the stars,
And cloak the earth in terror and gloom!
Come with Hunger and Desire,
And empower me with your timeless force!
I offer myself to be consumed in your harsh Vacuum,
Which swallows worlds and feeds on souls of the living!
My body is a vessel for your formless essence!
Come from the Black City of Pyramids,
From alien wastelands and empty spaces,
And grant me the power to destroy those who oppose me!
Rip their hearts and devour their flesh!
Feast on the souls of my enemies,
And plague them with sickness and misery!
Burn their eyes so that they may not see the Light,
And leave them screaming in agony of fear and despair!
Enter this Temple of Flesh,
Forge my Soul through your fearsome rites of abomination,
And intoxicate my dreams with visions of primordial Void!
I invoke you in the name of the Dragon!
In Nomine Draconis!
Ho Drakon Ho Megas!

Burn the parchment with the sigil and let the smoke carry your invocation through the planes. Envision how the gates of your soul open up to receive the essence of the spirit and enter the trance of possession. Let your consciousness merge with the energies of the demon through sexual ecstasy or use the visual meditation provided below. Uridimmu enters the flesh as a swirling vortex of energy. The practitioner is suddenly enveloped with dense black smoke, wrapping around and suffocating. The heart pounds, you feel dizzy and you cannot breathe. When the possession is complete, the mind is filled with black atavistic energy, primal hunger for life force and vital essence. You may now let the vision flow freely and explore the powers of the spirit, which are yours to command, or you may focus the energies upon a specific target. Uridimmu endows the practitioner with the power to send a black, destructive wind through the planes. Empowered by invoked force, envision yourself in the form of the demon and channel the energies upon the target in the form of black lashes, harsh and burning. Visualize how dense clouds of black energy wrap around the victim, consuming the soul and scorching the flesh, until the whole vital force is devoured. When you wish to end the working, return to your mundane consciousness, thank the spirit, and close the rite.

MEDITATION: PYRAMID TEMPLE

Envision yourself in the black desert, which looks like wasteland where everything was burnt to the ground. The sand reminds you of ashes. The whole landscape looks alien, more like a strange planet than any place on the earth. In the distance, you can see a huge complex of towers and pyramids, all black, emanating purple mist which cloaks the whole scenery. The buildings and constructions do not resemble anything made by human hands. You are walking towards the first pyramid in which you notice an open door, shining with purple light from the inside. As you enter the building, you realize that this is a temple and there is a round altar in the centre of the chamber. It seems to be made of dense black energy, forming a flat surface with black tentacles and tendrils writhing around. You also seem to notice numerous eyes opening and blinking in this strange mass of shadow energy. Undress and lie on the altar. You can feel streaks of shadow shooting out from all around and penetrating you through all chakras and sensory organs. This feels ecstatic and sexual. Suddenly, your consciousness splits and you realize that you are standing by the altar and looking at yourself, naked and exposed, and you are holding a knife. Start stabbing your body on the altar, drink the blood and feast on the flesh. Let your blood flow onto the altar and feed it with your life essence. Now, you feel more empowered and ecstatic than ever before. Let the vision flow freely or use the invoked energy for other magical work.

DREAM WORK: THE BLACK DESERT

Focus on the sigil of Uridimmu before going to sleep and chant the name of the demon until you sense his presence in the room. When the atmosphere is slightly charged with the black energies of the spirit, trace the Key of the Night in front of you and recite the words of dream invocation:

In the name of Tiamat,
I stir the Black Waters of the Abyss,
And I lift the Veil of the Night
To gaze into mysteries which lie beyond the world of Waking.
In the name of the Mother,
I call Uridimmu to be my guide and companion through dreams and
nightmares.
By the Key of the Night I open the Gateways to Dreamlands,
And I seek to rest in the Arms of the Dragon,
In a dream which will take me to the Heart of the Void,
To the Lost Desert where I will meet the Wolf Demon,
The messenger of Those who dwell beyond the stars.
So it shall be!

Place the sigil below the pillow, lie down on the bed and close your eyes. Envision a door with the symbol of the spirit shining with dim purple light. The door opens and you are invited to walk through. Focus on visualization given below and let yourself fall asleep, keeping your mind focused on the intent of continuing the vision in a dream.

When you walk through the door, visualize yourself in the desert again. It is nighttime, the whole scenery is pitch black and you can barely see anything around. There is no moon and no stars and the sky above resembles black cosmic void or a completely empty space. In the distance, you notice a shape of a living creature moving in the surrounding darkness. It looks like a beast but you cannot tell whether it is a lion, a wolf, or something different. Start chanting the name of the demon. After a while, you will feel a strange wind rising around you, black and dense. It is dancing and swirling, assuming shapes and forms which eventually crystallize into an entity which looks like a human being, but his face resembles a wolf or a lion and has the yellow eyes of a beast. His skin is dark and there is something inhuman about the creature. Ask him to be your guide through this black landscape and let the vision continue in your dreams.

DRACONIAN SIGIL OF URIDIMMU

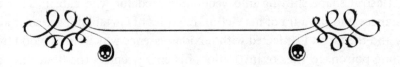

GIRTABLULLÛ

DESCRIPTION, ORIGIN AND MAGICAL POWERS

The Scorpion Man is the title ascribed to the creature mentioned in the *Enuma Elish* as Girtablullû or Akrabamêlu. In Akkadian art, he is depicted with a human head, bird's legs, a snake-headed penis and a scorpion's body and tail. Sometimes, he also has wings. In artwork of later periods, such creatures commonly appear alongside the Sun God and the linguistic part –*lullû* usually denotes a human upper body. The legend of Gilgamesh mentions a scorpion-man and a scorpion-woman as guardians of the mountain where the sun rises and sets, yet from a magical point of view these entities are distinct from the spirit described in the *Enuma Elish*. In early mythology, Girtablullû manipulated heavenly bodies with its pincers and was identified with the constellation of Sagittarius.

In works of magic, Girtablullû appears either as a huge black scorpion or as a half-man half-scorpion, with human upper body. He endows the practitioner with the power to use spiritual "venom," both in rites of self-empowerment and in hostile sorcery, and he holds the keys to transformation of consciousness through ecstasy of pain and pleasure. This is related to the art of astral shape-shifting into venomous predator who can inject toxic substances into the aura of his victim. Energies of Girtablullû are solar and fiery and the target is infected with noxious essence which turns blood into burning poison. In rites of invocation, his energy enters the flesh through the solar plexus and spreads onto other bodily parts, inducing transformation, which is experienced at first as agonizing pain but then it changes into ecstasy. This is often accompanied by visions of being torn to pieces and re-created with the very flesh of the demon, or bleeding out on the altar in the temple of Girtablullû, while blood is being replaced by the spirit's venom. Because of this poisonous power he might perhaps be associated with the Samael qlipha which contains the chalice of spiritual poison and is called "The Venom of God."

Girtablullû is also the guardian of forgotten knowledge and forbidden gnosis of lost civilizations. His temples are hidden underground and buried deep beneath the desert sands, on the Other Side of the world. He appears when the sun disappears behind the horizon, emerging from the Gate of Sunset. He is the lord of all creatures that dwell underground and hide from the burning sun but walk upon the surface of the earth when the stars shine in the sky, crawling out of their abode in black pits and dark caves. His temples are buried under the desert and hidden among rocks and mountains, and can be accessed through the gate of the setting sun or through portals of timeless sands. They are carved inside huge black rocks and decorated with golden ornaments. He dwells in deserted cities inhabited only by phantoms and undead, where blood flows in fountains and aqueducts instead of water. When summoned, he appears with the army of monsters, scorpions or half-men half-scorpions forming from sands and rocks. Girtablullû, himself, arises from the desert sands, forming into a venomous black scorpion who rules the desert at night. Sometimes, he has a ball of fire at the end of his tail with which he can crush and burn those who get in his way. But apart from the scorpion, he also assumes the shape of a dragon. In this form, he rules the powers of the rising sun which destroy civilizations and burn the living. This is the dawn heralding the apocalypse, the ultimate end of the cosmic cycle.

THE EYE OF THE SCORPION

EVOCATION

Trace the lines of the sigil with your own blood, chanting the name of the demon in low whispering voice. Place a few drops of blood on the ritual blade and trace the Key of the Night in the air above the mirror. An ordinary black mirror will be most suitable for this working. Envision the Key glimmering with dim, fiery light, and drawing energies from the Other Side into the Temple. Make the offering of life energies or your sexual fluids, sending the intent of the ritual through the planes. When you feel ready to begin the summoning, recite the words of conjuration:

I call you, Guardian of Lost Knowledge and Ancient Mysteries!
I call you, Scorpion Man!
I summon you, Girtablullû, to manifest in this Temple!
Awaken from your sleep in forgotten shrines,
Beneath the blood-dyed desert,
Arise to me through the Gate of Sunset,
And bring the dawn as the world has never seen!
Come from deserted cities and lost civilizations,
With burning rays of the rising sun,
And unleash the dreadful force of the Apocalypse!
I open the Gates of the Night,
To call you forth, Venomous Scorpion!
Arise from oceans of blood,
With light that brings nothingness,
Clothed with fire and smoke,

In glorious terror of the Primal Void!
I, ... (your magical name), call you, Girtablullû, to come and
manifest!
Come to me and assist me in my Work,
Grant me the fulfillment of my Desire which I seek to accomplish,
Which is .... (state the intent of the rite).
Let my Will be done!
I call you by the Key of the Night which opens the Gates and removes
boundaries between the worlds,
I call you by the power of my blood which is the essence of the
Dragon,
And I call you in the name of the Dragon,
In Nomine Tiamat
Ho Ophis Ho Archaios
Ho Drakon Ho Megas!

Focus on the mirror and chant the name of the demon in low whispering voice. Visualize the sigil forming on the black surface, glowing with dim fire, surrounded by smoke. Envision how the mirror becomes a living portal and how the energies of the Other Side are flowing into the Temple. When you notice the spirit manifesting into visible shape in the mirror gateway, communicate with the demon. When this is finished, thank the spirit and close the working with the words:

In the name of the Dragon,
This is my Will and so it shall be!

Girtablullû manifests in the Temple with tangible presence. The air grows hot and becomes suffocating, tongues of astral fire surround the altar and shadows flicker on the walls. Smoke flows through the mirror and intoxicates the practitioner with poisonous vapors, inducing dreamy trance and transforming mundane perception. When evoked to visible form, he appears as a strong, muscular man, with pitch-black skin, but his demeanor is rather unearthly, not displaying any ethnic features. His eyes are empty black holes and he is surrounded by the aura of dread and terror, as if he was a venomous scorpion dressed in human skin. He may also appear in the form described in mythological sources, with human torso and scorpion's tail and legs. Sometimes, instead of arms he has scorpion's pincers. He also manifests in the shape of a huge black scorpion, but this form is more suitable for works of invocation. While other demons may specifically ask for a sacrifice of life in which the blood is spilt in their name and the soul is offered to empower their manifestations, Girtablullû prefers the vital essence of the conjuror to other offerings. In rites of malediction, he rips the aura and injects his venom into victim's blood. The venom spreads over the whole body in burning agony, poisoning the flesh and causing damage to spiritual centers. This results in general weakness and fatigue, blood disorders, swellings, muscle twitching and convulsions. Girtablullû strikes fast and his venom is lethal. His attack causes numbness and paralysis, making the victim helpless and unable to use defensive mechanisms. When focused on the target, his essence is a truly deadly weapon.

INVOCATION

Open the ritual with placing a few drops of your own blood on the parchment with the sigil of the demon or trace the lines of the glyph with your vital essence. With a blooded ritual blade, draw the Key of the Night in front of you above the altar and visualize how it shines with dim, fiery light, while the Temple is being filled with dark, intoxicating smoke. Gaze for a while into the sigil of the demon, chanting his name in low whisper, and envision how the glyph becomes alive, activated by the venomous energy of Girtablullû. When the atmosphere in the Temple is charged, recite the words of invocation:

> *By the Blood of the Dragon which is my own Essence,*
> *And by the Key of the Night,*
> *I call you, Girtablullû!*
> *Fearsome Scorpion Man,*
> *Guardian of Arcane Knowledge and Forbidden Secrets!*
> *Come to me, Fierce Lord of the Desert,*
> *And cloak me in your venomous essence!*
> *Arise from deserted cities beneath the sands of time,*
> *With your army of scorpions,*
> *And empower me with your primordial Terror!*
> *Enter this flesh which I offer you as Temple,*
> *Poison my blood and replace it with your Venom,*
> *Through the rites of your noxious alchemy!*
> *Hear my call and come to me!*

Inspire and bless me with your timeless wisdom,
Reveal to me secrets of your intoxicating ecstasy,
And let me taste your dreadful essence from within!
Grant me the power to destroy my enemies,
Rip their flesh and devour their souls,
Paralyze their limbs so that they could not strike back,
And let their blood turn into burning poison!
Enter this Temple of Flesh,
Inject your seething Venom into my Soul,
And intoxicate my dreams with thirst for lost knowledge!
I invoke you in the name of the Dragon!
In Nomine Draconis!
Ho Drakon Ho Megas!

Let your invocation arise through the planes when you burn the parchment with the sigil, sending the intent of the ritual through the medium of smoke. Then let your consciousness merge with the venomous essence of the spirit in ecstatic possession. Use the visual meditation given below or take your soul to the gates of flesh through the trance of sexual ecstasy. Enflame yourself to the point in which your soul will ascend beyond the boundaries of bodily senses and feel how your blood, your vital essence, is being replaced by the energy of the demon. This is a burning and agonizing sensation which may hurt for a while, but then you will no longer feel the difference between pleasure and pain. You may let the vision flow freely, enjoying the communion with the spirit and exploring his powers, or you may focus his venomous energies upon a specific target. This transformation has a lasting effect on consciousness and after the ritual you may feel as if you were a scorpion in human skin. This effect may last for hours, days or even longer. If you wish to use the force of Girtablullû for magical attack, envision yourself in the scorpion form and strike the target with the spirit's venom, injecting it into the solar plexus and visualizing how it spreads over the whole body, or channel the draconian essence of the demon and burn the victim with your flaming breath. When you wish to finish the working, return to your mundane consciousness, thank the spirit, and close the rite.

MEDITATION: BLACK SCORPION

Envision yourself in a desert. The sun is setting, but it is still extremely hot and the sand burns your naked feet. Suddenly, the desert sands rise and begin to crystallize into a huge scorpion. At first, it looks as if it is made of sand, but then, it turns completely black. He is now alive and moves in your direction. He bites you in the forehead, in your third eye. You fall on the ground, feeling the venom flowing through your veins and spreading onto the whole body. It is extremely painful, but after a while, you get used to pain and you watch how your flesh is transforming. You change into half-scorpion. A thick black shell grows over your body and your eyes turn yellow and start to glow. You also realize that you can use this venom for any purpose you wish. This astral form is suitable both for protection and for works of *malefica*. You can use it to travel through the astral plane with no fear of any aggressors. It can also be used for magical attack. Explore the nature of both qualities, let the visions flow freely or experiment with this shape-shifting meditation as a preliminary working to other magical operations.

DREAM WORK: DESERT TEMPLE

Before going to sleep, focus for a while on the sigil of Girtablullû and chant the name of the demon. You can use the primary sigil or the eye portal with scorpions. When you sense the presence of the spirit and the atmosphere is intoxicated with his venomous essence, trace the Key of the Night in front of you and speak the words of dream invocation:

> *In the name of Tiamat,*
> *I stir the Black Waters of the Abyss,*
> *And I lift the Veil of the Night*
> *To gaze into mysteries which lie beyond the world of Waking.*
> *In the name of the Mother,*
> *I call Girtablullû to be my guide and companion through dreams*
> *and nightmares.*
> *By the Key of the Night I open the Gateways to Dreamlands,*
> *And I seek to rest in the Arms of the Dragon,*
> *In a dream which will take me to the lost city in the desert,*
> *Where I shall walk with the Scorpion God,*
> *Among those who carry the blood of the Dragon.*
> *So it shall be!*

Place the sigil below the pillow, lie down on the bed and close your eyes. Envision a door with the symbol of the spirit and visualize it glowing with dim fiery light. The door opens and you are invited to walk through. Focus on visualization given below and let yourself fall asleep with your mind focused on the intent of continuing the vision in a dream.

When you walk through the door of sleep, visualize yourself standing in a desert. It is dark and you shiver from cold. In the distance, but close enough to see the outlines, there is an ancient stone city carved in the rocky desert mountains. The atmosphere is quite ominous and you can hear the howling of hyenas. When you look up, you see hungry vultures circling above you. You walk slowly towards the city, passing scattered bones of men and animals, skeletons and half-decayed corpses of other travelers, which are now the feasting ground for the vultures. Suddenly, you are surrounded by thousands of small scorpions which appear somewhere from beneath. They swarm around you and bite you one by one, and when you fall dead on the ground, your flesh is immediately devoured and there are only bones left. You look down on them and realize that you are now pure energy, existing only in your spiritual form. Now, you can enter the city. You reach the gateway carved in stone, and when you walk through the door, you find yourself in a huge hallway. There is a large throne in the centre and you see the demon in his scorpion form. He has human torso, bearded head with a tiara, legs and claws of a bird, scorpion's tail and penis with the snake head. Ask him to be your guide through the realm of dreams and explore the city when you fall asleep.

Draconian sigil of Girtablullû

Ūmu Dabrūtu

DESCRIPTION, ORIGIN AND MAGICAL POWERS

Ūmu Dabrūtu, also called the "Mighty Tempests" or the "Fierce Storm-Demon," is another entity associated with weather phenomena. Historical sources are uncertain about the appearance of the spirit, though it is suggested that it might have incorporated certain features of a lion, accordingly to other personifications of violent weather.

In rites of magic, this spirit often appears as a swirling vortex of Chaos with a burning eye in the centre. The eye is either fiery or yellow and resembles eyes of an animal or beast. On other occasions, Ūmu Dabrūtu assumes the form of a black tornado, a very violent and destructive vortex of energy. When invoked, the vortex is absorbed into consciousness through the third eye on the forehead and the practitioner becomes the eye of the tornado, the central axis of the energy. This is experienced as a powerful surge of wrath and aggression, a strong wave of emotions which can be focused and directed for magical purposes. It is an aggressive, but also joyful and invigorating experience. When used in malefic sorcery, the force of the demon brings chaos and havoc into the life of a person, manifesting in phenomena of the surrounding world and disrupting their natural balance. The practitioner can channel and direct the destructive vortex both through rites of evocation and invocation.

Both Ūmu Dabrūtu and Ugallu in source literature are referred to as hurricanes, tornadoes, storms and raging winds. They are associated with violent forces of nature, roaring oceans, rains and hail, floods, earthquakes, and other natural disasters. They also both manifest with lightning and thunder, assuming the form of an astral vortex which tears through boundaries between the worlds. But, while the domain of Ugallu is air and electricity, the energy of Ūmu Dabrūtu is fiery and so are his manifestations on material plane. He comes with bolts of lightning, but in their essence, they are bolts of liquid fire. He often appears as living fire and when invoked, he can transform the astral form of the practitioner into a fire elemental or a fiery phoenix with flaming wings.

Ūmu Dabrūtu inspires dreams of flying, either with winds and hurricanes or on the wings of a phoenix, but always soaring very high and very fast. It is a very dynamic force of movement and change. When compared to the qlipothic Tree of Night, it would be most suitable to connect this demon with the violent and fiery sphere of Golachab.

THE EYE OF THE STORM

EVOCATION

Open the ritual with chanting the name of the demon while the sigil is activated by being traced with your own blood. Then, place a few drops of blood on the ritual blade and draw the Key of the Night in the air above the mirror. Envision the Key shining with liquid fire and visualize fiery Draconian energies flowing from the Other Side into the Temple. Make the offering of life energies or your sexual fluids, sending the intent of the rite through the planes. When you feel ready to begin the conjuration, speak the words of summoning:

> *I call you, Fierce Storm Demon who comes with fire and lightning,*
> *I call you, Mighty Tempests!*
> *I summon you, Ūmu Dabrūtu, to manifest in this Temple!*
> *Arise from the Eye of Chaos,*
> *Through the Fiery Gateway,*
> *With living flames that destroy and transform!*
> *Come from beyond Time,*
> *With roaring hurricanes and raging winds,*
> *And bring the dread fire from the skies!*
> *I open the Gates of the Night,*
> *To call you forth, Raging Storm that none can withstand!*

Come with bolts of lightning and burning lashes,
Which tear the flesh of the earth,
And stand before me in your primal terror,
Clothed with blazing fury and fiery chaos!
I, ... (your magical name), call you, Ūmu Dabrūtu, to come and
manifest!
Come to me and assist me in my Work,
Grant me the fulfillment of my Desire which I seek to accomplish,
Which is .... (state the intent of the rite).
Let my Will be done!
I call you by the Key of the Night which opens the Gates and removes
boundaries between the worlds,
I call you by the power of my blood which is the essence of the
Dragon,
And I call you in the name of the Dragon,
In Nomine Tiamat
Ho Ophis Ho Archaios
Ho Drakon Ho Megas!

Gaze into the mirror and chant the name of the demon. Cry it out into the Void and envision the sigil manifesting in the mirror, shining with liquid fire and swirling. Feel how the mirror becomes a gateway, activated by the vortex of energy flowing through the sigil. Ūmu Dabrūtu is very chaotic and has to be specifically asked to manifest in a shape allowing for communication. Otherwise, he will appear as a vortex of fire and lightning. When you notice the demon crystallizing into visible form in the black gateway, communicate with the spirit. When communication is finished, thank the demon and close the ritual with the words:

In the name of the Dragon,
This is my Will and so it shall be!

Ūmu Dabrūtu manifests within the mirror, but his presence is also sensed in the whole Temple. His energy is vast and without distinct boundaries, which makes the ritual of evocation quite a challenge. He hardly appears in any anthropomorphic form and communication on the ordinary level is not always possible. He usually comes as a shapeless vortex of energy, consisting of bolts of lightning and tongues of flame, or as a tentacle creature with wings of fire. On very rare occasions, he may appear in human shape, as an old, skinny man with fiery eyes and windy hair, emerging from clouds of black smoke. His manifestations, however, are very tangible and powerful. His presence is signaled by sensations of fire and smoke. The air in the Temple turns hot and dry, you can feel the scorching heat, smell the stench of burning, and hear the flames crackling around. His essence is fiery and apart from the mirror, it is recommended to evoke him through the medium of fire, especially if the rite is conducted outdoors. His energy also intensifies during storms and tempests. In rites of malediction, Ūmu Dabrūtu attacks with the speed of lightning and the force of a tornado. He strikes the target with fiery lightning, through the solar plexus, and creates a vortex of highly destructive energy which spreads over the whole body, causing damage to the aura and spiritual centers. The vortex also draws energies of chaos and entropy into the life of the victim, disrupting mundane reality and wreaking havoc all around. These energies manifest through the phenomena of the external world, replacing harmony and balance with chaos and misery. Health, prosperity, relationships, etc. are replaced by sickness, isolation, and all sorts of failures and misfortunes, flowing with the force of a hurricane which cannot be stopped or banished.

INVOCATION

Draw the sigil of the demon on a piece of parchment and activate it with your own blood, by placing a few drops on the sigil or by tracing the lines of the glyph. With a blooded ritual blade, draw the Key of the Night in front of you above the altar, and visualize it glowing with radiant flames, empowering the Temple with the fiery essence of the spirit. Focus on the sigil, chanting the name of the demon, and envision how the glyph becomes alive, shining with liquid fire and drawing the energy into your consciousness. When the Temple is charged and you feel ready to begin the ritual, recite the words of invocation:

> By the Blood of the Dragon which is my own Essence,
> And by the Key of the Night,
> I call you, Ūmu Dabrūtu!
> Fearsome Demon of Blazing Chaos!
> Furious Tempests and Raging Storms!
> Come through the Gateway of Fire,
> Arise from Primordial Void,

with flames and lightning,
Scourging the earth and devouring the stars!
I offer myself to be consumed in your burning ecstasy,
Enter my flesh and transform me from within,
In the rites of your fearsome alchemy!
Strike the world with primal terror!
And rise in agony of tortured souls!
Hear my call and come to me!
Grant me the power to crush mankind and human creations!
Emblaze my soul with living fire,
and fortify me with your furious essence!
Burn my enemies with your flaming lashes,
And leave them screaming with millions of tortured voices!
Enter this Temple of Flesh,
Lift my Soul in delirious flight,
Over the ruins of the world,
And enflame my dreams with Chaos and Fury!
I invoke you in the name of the Dragon!
In Nomine Draconis!
Ho Drakon Ho Megas!

Burn the parchment with the sigil and let your invocation rise through the planes with the smoke. Enter the trance of possession through the visual meditation provided below or by means of sexual ecstasy. Feel how the essence of the spirit expands your consciousness and how it enters your body through the third eye, burning the shape of the sigil on your forehead. You may also wish to paint the glyph on your forehead before the ritual in order to provide a focal point for the energy. Let your consciousness merge with the spirit's essence in ecstatic trance and open your mind for the boundless power of the demon. At this point, you may let the vision flow freely and explore the powers and energies of the spirit, or you may focus the force upon a target. Enflame yourself with rage and fury and strike your victim through solar plexus, visualizing damage within and without. Envision a black vortex swirling in the center of the target's body, exposing the victim to energies of chaos and entropy. Feel the ecstasy of aggression mixed with joy and excitement. When you wish to end the working, return to your mundane consciousness, thank the spirit, and close the ritual. You must remember, however, that the energy of Ūmu Dabrūtu is highly difficult to command

and master. He does not only strike the target, but also affects the immediate surroundings, family, friends, pets, etc. It is like trying to destroy one house in the whole city by means of a tornado. The force will eventually reach the target but the damage might be much greater than expected. It is, therefore, not recommended to use this demon in attacks focused on a singular person.

MEDITATION: EYE OF TORNADO

Envision yourself in a gloomy scene – heavy, black clouds hang above you. There is strange silence around and the atmosphere feels like before a heavy storm. After a moment, you hear a rolling thunder and you notice flashes of lightning in the distance. Suddenly, the silence is broken by loud howling of the wind and black tornado rises from the horizon. In the beginning, it seems small, but as it gets closer, it grows bigger and bigger until finally, it is huge and moving rapidly as it consumes everything in its way. You can see it coming in your direction, tearing trees from the ground and wreaking havoc on the land. In the centre of the tornado, there is an eye burning with bright, green light. Shortly after, the black vortex is so close that you are pulled inside. It feels like being struck by a powerful wave of energy. At first, you are moving with the swirling vortex, but you slow down until you are floating while still in the very eye of the tornado. You are the centre and the part of this enormous energy. And you realize you can control it. This is the vortex of astral chaos and it is extremely destructive. Let yourself merge with this essence and explore its powers by letting the vision flow freely or by focusing them on a target.

DREAM WORK: PORTAL OF FIRE

Before going to sleep, focus on the sigil of Ūmu Dabrūtu and chant the name of the demon. When you sense the presence of the spirit, trace the Key of the Night in front of you and speak the words of dream invocation:

In the name of Tiamat,
I stir the Black Waters of the Abyss,
And I lift the Veil of the Night
To gaze into mysteries which lie beyond the world of Waking.
In the name of the Mother,
I call Ūmu Dabrūtu to be my guide and companion through dreams
and nightmares.

By the Key of the Night I open the Gateways to Dreamlands,
And I seek to rest in the Arms of the Dragon,
In a dream which will take me to forgotten landscapes,
Where I shall soar through the worlds on the fiery wings of a
phoenix.
So it shall be!

Place the sigil below the pillow and lie down on the bed. Close your eyes and envision a door with the symbol of the spirit. The sigil glows with liquid fire. After a while, the door opens and you are invited to walk through. Focus on visualization given below and fall asleep, with your mind focused on the intent of continuing the vision in a dream.

When you walk through the door, visualize yourself standing on top of a mountain. The scenery is dark and gloomy. The sun is setting and stars appear on the firmament. All seems quiet, but suddenly, you notice a fiery phoenix soaring up in the sky. When it flies above you, he changes into a huge ball of fire and lightning which falls down and hits the ground. After a while, the fire burns out and the smoke crystallizes into human figure. It is an old skinny man with windy hair and fiery eyes, his essence is black smoke. He approaches you and touches your forehead, on your third eye. At this moment you feel that you are dissolving. You become liquid fire yourself and you fly up to the sky as a phoenix. You can soar in the air, you can breathe fire and burn all that stands in your way with the fiery essence. You can also burn everything with your touch and you can cast lightning with your eyes. This is an ecstatic feeling of total power. Keep it while falling asleep and fly as a phoenix through the realm of dreams.

DRACONIAN SIGIL OF ŪMU DABRŪTU

Kulullû

Description, origin and magical powers

The name Kulullû or Kulilu is translated as "the fish-man." Such creatures commonly appear in ancient Babylonian artwork, usually in male and female pairs, with human upper part of the body and the tail of a fish. They are associated with the water god, Ea, dwell in the watery abyss below the earth, and correspond to mermaids and mermen of European legends. However, the word, *kulullû*, might be related to several other Akkadian words denoting a female entity, and for this reason, the actual nature of the spirit from the *Enuma Elish* is uncertain. It is sometimes called a fish-centaur and identified with the constellation of Aquarius, the water-bearer.

Within works of magic, Kulullû arises from rivers and lakes of blood and appears as a demonic female with a fish tail, or in the form of a black hybrid with parts of spider and shellfish. She also has black tentacles, which resemble eels, but are covered with short hair that resemble the legs of a spider. She is connected with watery abysses, underwater temples and extremely bloody cults. Her powers represent the principle of death and decay, cosmic entropy and purification of consciousness through putrefaction. She inspires dreams about underground caves and underwater temples with cruel ceremonies in which her priestesses murder male sacrificial victims while copulating with them, feeding the demon with their flesh and their blood. When invoked, she devours the practitioner in an erotic union, which is experienced as being immersed in filth and decaying blood, suffocating or drowning in black water filled with rotten corpses. This is accompanied by atavistic sensations, affecting thoughts, feelings and emotions. Even the breath and natural physiology of the organism slow down and it feels like the whole flesh is falling into pieces, transformed by the black essence of the demon.

In magical warfare, Kulullû teaches the practitioner how to send out energy in the form of watery predators which devour the life-force of a victim and leave the body empty as a shell. She is venomous and bloodthirsty, feeding on vital essence and sexual energies. She incites thoughts of murder and bloody fantasies. She also feeds on dreams of the victim, transforming them into unbearable nightmares. When evoked to visible form, she strikes the target with her venom, thrusting tentacles into the subtle body of the victim. In rites of invocation, she fills the practitioner's consciousness with cold, emotionless stillness, which keeps the mind focused and ruthless towards the target. On the qlipothic Tree of Night, Kulullû might be associated with the Satariel qlipha, the level ruled by the demon-whore of the Qlipoth, the Saturnian sphere of death and decay.

THE EYE OF THE SPIDER

EVOCATION

Open the ritual by tracing the lines of the sigil with your blood and chanting the name of the demon. When this is done, place a few drops of blood on the ritual blade and draw the Key of the Night in the air above the mirror. Envision how the Key starts to glow with dim red light, drawing the energies of the Other Side into the Temple. Make the offering of life energies and your sexual fluids, sending the intent of the rite through the planes. In rites of Kulullû both a sacrifice of life and sexual energies is necessary. When you feel ready to begin the conjuration, speak the words of summoning:

I call you, Fish Demon who feeds of flesh and souls of the living,
I call you, Timeless Spirit of Death and Decay,
I summon you, Kulullû, to manifest in this Temple!
Awaken from your slumber in the Womb of the Dragon,
Arise from abysmal depths,
Beneath dead seas and black oceans!
Come with your dreadful breath of entropy,
Which dissolves the foundations of the world,
And stir the black waters of the Void!

I open the Gates of the Night,
To call you forth, Venomous Demon of Rot and Putrefaction!
Come forth with your festering essence,
With your primal hunger for life-force and vital powers!
Arise with nightmares and abominations,
From cold temples in the land of desolation,
And stand before me cloaked in tongues of black fire,
Lusting for the souls of the weak!
I, ... (your magical name), call you, Kulullû, to come and manifest!
Come to me and assist me in my Work,
Grant me the fulfillment of my Desire which I seek to accomplish,
Which is .... (state the intent of the rite).
Let my Will be done!
I call you by the Key of the Night which opens the Gates and removes
boundaries between the worlds,
I call you by the power of my blood which is the essence of the
Dragon,
And I call you in the name of the Dragon,
In Nomine Tiamat
Ho Ophis Ho Archaios
Ho Drakon Ho Megas!

Focus now on the mirror and chant the name of the demon. Visualize the sigil glowing red and dripping blood as it manifests on the black surface, and see how the mirror becomes a living portal to the Other Side. It is recommended to use the water mirror for this working. When you see the demon crystallizing into visible shape in the black gateway, communicate with the entity. Kulullû is extremely bloodthirsty and she needs a sacrifice of a living being in order to manifest, otherwise, she will feed on the vital force of the conjuror. When communication is finished, thank the demon and close the working with the words:

In the name of the Dragon,
This is my Will and so it shall be!

In rites of evocation, Kulullû appears in female form, with a human upper part of the body and a fish tail. She has empty, black eyes and black tentacles instead of hair. She resembles Medusa, but is more sinister and more predatory. Sometimes, she is holding a fish in her mouth. She may also come in half-human, half-fish form, with no limbs and a lot of tentacles. The tentacles are hairy and look like a strange hybrid of octopus limbs and spider legs. Her essence is highly vampiric and the more blood is offered in sacrifice, the better effects are manifested through the ritual. The sacrifice of blood may be partially substituted by the offering of sexual fluids, which she accepts as willingly as life essence. Kulullû manifests in the Temple with the stench of rotting flesh or decaying blood in the air. The atmosphere grows ominous and the temperature drops by a few degrees. The sigil appears in the mirror or above the altar and drips dark red blood. In rites of hostile sorcery, Kulullû brings flesh-eating diseases, which cause the rotting of the body, infections, inflammations, poisoning and slow and painful chronic illnesses. Her essence works slowly, infecting the flesh and stealing the vital force of the victim in a long and harsh process. She strikes through the throat or through the mouth, thrusting her tentacles into the target's flesh. She feeds on the soul and life essence of the victim, which weakens the body, making it vulnerable to diseases and finally, kills the person in a slow and agonizing way.

INVOCATION

Place a few drops of your own blood on the parchment with the sigil of the demon or use the blood to trace the lines of the glyph. When this is done, anoint the ritual blade with your life essence and trace the Key of the Night in front of you, above the altar. Envision it shining with blood-red radiance, empowering the Temple with the energies of Kulullû. Gaze for a while into the sigil while chanting the name of the demon and see how the lines of the glyph become alive and glow with dim red light, empowered by the essence of the spirit. When the atmosphere in the Temple is charged and you feel ready to begin the ritual, speak the words of invocation:

> By the Blood of the Dragon which is my own Essence,
> And by the Key of the Night,
> I call you, Kulullû!
> Flesh Eating Demon!
> Venomous Spirit of Rot and Entropy!
> Arise from rivers of blood,
> And lost temples in the bowels of the earth.
> Come forth from winding labyrinths,

Where the dead feast on the living.
Arise from filth and decaying waters,
And fill the world with your venom and stench!
I offer my body as a vessel for your black essence,
And I seek to rise as your living manifestation!
Hear my call and come to me!
Awaken my hunger, thirst and desire!
Grant me the powers to command the forces of death,
To deliver plague, sickness and misery upon those who stand in my
way!
Unleash your horrible wrath upon my enemies,
Devour their souls and feast on their flesh,
And leave their tortured bodies empty as shells,
With maggots squirming in their rotting corpses!
Enter this Temple of Flesh,
Intoxicate my Soul with your festering essence,
And infect my dreams with visions of the arcane and the forbidden!
I call you in the name of the Dragon!
In Nomine Draconis!
Ho Drakon Ho Megas!

Burn the parchment with the sigil and let the smoke carry your invocation through the planes. Then, offer yourself to be consumed and transformed by the energies of the demon. Enter the trance of possession through sexual ecstasy and let it take you to the gates of exhaustion and beyond. You can also use the visual meditation given below. As your soul ascends beyond the boundaries of flesh, let your consciousness merge in communion with the essence of the spirit. You may let the vision flow freely, exploring the powers of the demon, which are now your own, or you may channel the energies upon a specific target. In works of protection and self-empowerment, Kulullû cloaks the practitioner with black, venomous essence, which absorbs magical attacks and dissolves hostile energies. If you wish to use the energy of the demon in malefic sorcery, invoke the force, envision yourself in the form of the spirit and thrust the astral tentacles into the subtle body of the target. With the tentacles, you can drain vital energies, which is a fast and deadly astral attack, but you can also inject the venom into spiritual centers of the victim, leaving the festering essence of the demon to work its way through the target's body, which causes flesh-rotting infections. With the force of Kulullû, you can also drown the sleeping victim in astral waters. The black poisonous essence enters the flesh through the subtle body, causing swellings and putrefaction from within. When you wish to end the working, return to your mundane consciousness, thank the spirit, and close the ritual. If your own spiritual body is not fortified enough with Draconian essence to withstand the energies of Kulullû, it might be advisable to cleanse yourself after the work with this entity because the invoked energy is very black and carries a strong essence of entropy, which may affect both the target and the practitioner.

MEDITATION: FISH LAKE

Envision yourself standing on the shore of a black lake in the middle of a swamp. Call the name of the demon and trace her sigil in the air. You will see a creature emerging from the lake. She is an entity in human form, but she has the tail of a fish and empty fish eyes. Instead of hair, she has black tentacles coming out of her head and writhing around. At first glance, they look like black eels, but they are not. The water in the lake is pitch black and pieces of rotting human and animal flesh are floating around. The stench of rot and decay is almost suffocating. The demon touches your forehead, gazing straight into your eyes and your consciousness merges with hers. You can feel your flesh transforming into a strange hybrid of half-human, half-fish, with hairy tentacles which resemble spider limbs. You are also being filled with the demon's essence which feels cold, deadly and focused. You can use this energy for astral attack, e.g. by sending out astral eels which enter the body of a victim through the throat or through the mouth and devour the vital force until there is nothing left, or by "drowning" the victim in black astral waters of putrefaction. Experiment with the powers of the demon or simply let the vision flow freely and open yourself for whatever may come.

DREAM WORK

Before going to sleep, focus for a while on the sigil of the demon and chant the name of the spirit. Both meditations provided below were designed to induce dreams inspired by Kulullû. When you feel the presence of the demon, trace The Key of the Night in front of you and speak the words of dream invocation:

In the name of Tiamat,
I stir the Black Waters of the Abyss,
And I lift the Veil of the Night
To gaze into mysteries which lie beyond the world of Waking.
In the name of the Mother,
I call Kulullû to be my guide and companion through dreams and
nightmares.
By the Key of the Night I open the Gateways to Dreamlands,
And I seek to rest in the Arms of the Dragon,
In a dream which will take me to lost lands and forgotten temples,
Where I shall join ancient rites of blood,
And taste the pleasures of forbidden ceremonies.
So it shall be!

Place the sigil below the pillow and lie down on the bed. Visualize a
black door with the symbol of the spirit. The glyph glows with dim red light
and drips dark red blood. Envision how the door opens and you are invited
to walk through. Focus on either of the following visualizations below and
let yourself fall asleep with your mind focused on the intent of continuing
the vision in a dream.

Forgotten Temple

Visualize yourself in an underwater scenery which looks like the bottom of
the sea or the ocean. Everything is green and blue and the water is cloudy.
Call the name of the demon. You will see a creature resembling a mixture
of a crab and a spider, completely black. The atmosphere is ominous and
slightly electrified. Follow the demon until she leads you to an underwater
cave, which is the entrance to a hidden temple. Above the gateway, there is a
female eye, alive and blinking. Walls are covered with hieroglyphs and each
of them contains the glyph of a circle. After walking through a long hallway,
you will reach the ritual chamber. There are priests and priestesses dressed
in long black robes. They have red eyes, large earlobes and gills on the necks.
By the wall, there is a round altar with human entrails, freshly torn from
sacrificial victims. In the centre of the chamber, you notice a round pool
with a huge black creature rising up from the water. Her mouth resembles
female genitals with sharp teeth, surrounded by black tentacles, opening up
to receive the sacrificial food and closing to digest it. The priests are feeding

her with the entrails from the altar. Join the ceremony and let the visions continue freely in your dreams.

Cave of Blood

Imagine yourself in a gloomy wasteland. It is calm and empty, as if there was no life around, no birds, no animals, not even insects. You are standing in front of a huge rock. Use your blood to paint the sigil of the demon on the rock and chant her name. The rock will crack, revealing the entrance to a cave. The cave is huge and the entrance looks like made of branches of a tree, but they are alive and resemble hairy spider legs. Above the entrance, there is also an eye, alive and moving. When you go inside, you notice that these hairy branches are all around and there is only small space in the center and no passage to go further. Beneath your feet you can see the roots of this strange tree which grow into the cave. Use your blood again – let a few drops fall on the roots and the ground will start moving down, like a lift, taking you to the Underworld. When it stops, you will find yourself in a huge, long tunnel, built around the river of blood. Call the name of the demon again. You will see a barque with a spectral ferryman who will take you to a portal of pulsating red light. While falling asleep, walk through the portal and explore the vision in your dreams.

DRACONIAN SIGIL OF KULULLÛ

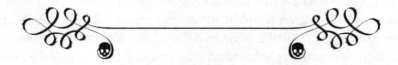

Kusarikku

Description, origin and magical powers

Kusarikku is mentioned in the *Enuma Elish* as the Bison-Man. In other historical sources and research literature, this creature is also known as *Gudalim*. Both terms originally denoted a bull-man or a man with a bull's head and they probably derived from the bison. In Akkadian and Babylonian art, this entity is usually associated with the Sun God, Shamash, along with Uridimmu. He holds door posts and emblems, often the sun-disc. He is sometimes presented as fighting other beasts, especially the lion-demon, which could refer to Uridimmu, and he is considered a protective entity, identified with the constellation of Capricorn.

In magical work, *Kusarikku* manifests as the Lord of the Desert and appears as a giant half-bull half-man – he has the head and legs of a bull, but human torso and arms. He is the ruler of the desert, the lord of burnt souls and he presides over all who died among the desert sands. Sometimes, he sits on a throne in a great temple made of sand among golden pyramids. His energy is solar and is often experienced through visions of the burning sun, or through sigils and glyphs based on solar imagery. His power is the primal force of creation, initiating dynamic movement, action, progress, and evolution. However, it is also very destructive and can be used for death magic, curses and other works of malediction.

When invoked, he enters the body and the soul in a surge of overwhelming, abstract and atavistic energy. Mundane perception is immediately swept away and human patterns of thinking are transformed into primal consciousness. This can literally deprive the practitioner of the ability to speak, write or express thoughts by verbal means for a certain time – e.g. a few hours or even a few days. He holds the power to shape the matter and the spirit, to transform the soul and to fortify the body with his boundless essence.

Kusarikku inspires dreams of the desert and primordial visions of creation and destruction, images of making golems from clay and breathing the spark of the soul into their mortal bodies, or pictures of wastelands and ruins of civilizations. On the qlipothic Tree of Night, he might perhaps be associated with the Thaumiel qlipha, along with the shadow-demon Uridimmu, with whom he is involved in an eternal fight, like two demonic rulers of Thaumiel – Satan and Moloch. Besides, the image of a bull might also correspond to mythological depictions of Moloch, deity widely worshipped in the Middle East, famous for human sacrifices burnt alive in sacred fire.

SIGIL OF THE LORD OF THE DEAD

EVOCATION

Open the ritual by tracing the lines of the sigil with a few drops of your own blood and chanting the name of the demon. Then, anoint the ritual blade and draw the Key of the Night in the air above the mirror. Water mirror is not recommended for this working. Envision the Key shining with golden fiery light and drawing the energies of the Other Side into the Temple. Make the offering of life energies or your sexual fluids and send the intent of the ritual through the planes. When you feel ready to begin the conjuration, recite the words of summoning:

> *I call you, Mighty Bull Demon who rules the Sands of Time,*
> *I call you, Lord of the Golden Desert!*
> *I summon you, Kusarikku, to manifest in this Temple!*
> *Arise from forgotten hallways and subterranean labyrinths,*
> *Where ancient fires burn on the altars,*
> *And where ritual places are filled with screams of sacrifices!*
> *Come from the land beyond Time,*
> *With glory and force,*
> *With horror and splendor,*
> *And summon your army of demons to rise at my command!*

I open the Gates of the Night,
To call you forth, Fearsome Bull of the Desert!
Raise the sands and gather the winds,
Let the world tremble before your timeless power!
And stand before me in your primal majesty,
With endless force of creation and destruction!
I, ... (your magical name), call you, Kusarikku, to come and
manifest!
Come to me and assist me in my Work,
Grant me the fulfillment of my Desire which I seek to accomplish,
Which is .... (state the intent of the rite).
Let my Will be done!
I call you by the Key of the Night which opens the Gates and removes
boundaries between the worlds,
I call you by the power of my blood which is the essence of the
Dragon,
And I call you in the name of the Dragon,
In Nomine Tiamat
Ho Ophis Ho Archaios
Ho Drakon Ho Megas!

When the words are spoken, gaze into the mirror, chant the name of the demon and envision how the black surface becomes a living gateway for the energies of the Other Side. Visualize the sigil manifesting in the gateway, shining with warm golden light and flickering with tongues of golden fire. When you notice the demon crystallizing into visible shape in the mirror, communicate with the entity. His essence is very atavistic and his message is often received through non-verbal means. He may choose to speak to you but you should rather focus on visions, impulses, feelings and emotions – this is how abstract experience is translated by the inner mind into your personal language. When communication is finished, thank the spirit and close the rite with the words:

In the name of the Dragon,
This is my Will and so it shall be!

Kusarikku appears as half-man half-bull. His head and the lower part of the body are shaped like a bull, but he has human torso and arms, like a mythical Minotaur. As the Lord of the Desert, he manifests in human form with a horned golden helmet on his head, covering the face and he is holding a spear in his hand. He commands an army of golems which arise from desert sands and are destroyed by water. When evoked for works of death and malediction, he appears in a long black robe and with a bull's skull instead of the head. Sometimes, he holds a large diamond-shaped ruby in his hands. When he comes to the Temple, the temperature rises by a few degrees and the air grows dry and slightly suffocating. His tremendous energy cannot be contained within a focal point and his presence is sensed all around. His seething breath enters the room like hot wind and the walls tremble when he manifests in the Temple. If the ritual is conducted outdoors, he shakes the earth and summons the winds to rise as he shapes into visible form before the conjuror. In hostile sorcery, Kusarikku teaches the practitioner how to use the hot and dry energy to deprive a person of life-force and to make the body crumble into dust. He may also crush the victim in his deadly embrace, but his powers are abstract to human consciousness and very difficult to focus and handle.

INVOCATION

Place a few drops of your own blood upon the sigil of the demon or trace the lines of the glyph with your life essence. Take the ritual blade anointed with blood and draw the Key of the Night in front of you, above the altar. Visualize how it shines with golden fire, empowering the Temple with Draconian energies. Gaze for a while into the sigil, while chanting the name of the demon, and envision how the glyph becomes alive, activated by the primal essence of Kusarikku. When the Temple is charged, and you feel ready to begin the ritual, speak the words of invocation:

> *By the Blood of the Dragon which is my own Essence,*
> *And by the Key of the Night,*
> *I call you, Kusarikku!*
> *Fearsome Bull Demon!*
> *Ancient Lord of Burnt Souls!*
> *Arise from the Sands of Time,*
> *From forgotten deserts and barren wastelands,*
> *With abominations of the earth,*
> *And with monsters born in the Great Below.*
> *Summon your harsh winds and crush the world,*

Treading upon the ruins of civilizations!
I offer myself to be transformed and forged
In the furnace of your timeless flames,
Through the mysteries of your primal alchemy.
Come with unspeakable horrors of the Lost Desert,
Awaken those who sleep in hidden places,
And grant me the powers of creation and destruction!
Deliver death and misfortune upon my enemies,
Take away their vital force,
Burn their cursed souls,
And let their mortal bodies crumble to dust!
Enter this Temple of Flesh,
Let my Soul rise on your seething breath,
And enflame my dreams with hunger and terror of the Void!
I invoke you in the name of the Dragon!
In Nomine Draconis!
Ho Drakon Ho Megas!

Burn the parchment with the sigil and let your desire of communion with the spirit arise through the planes with the smoke. When this is done, enter the trance of possession and let your consciousness merge with the atavistic essence of the demon. Use the visual meditation given below or enflame yourself in sexual ecstasy. Kusarikku enters the flesh in forceful, aggressive possession, which feels like being crushed by waves of energy pressing from all around. A rapid surge of tremendous heat spreads over the whole body in burning agony, which is extremely painful and overwhelming, but then the soul is lifted in ecstasy beyond the gates of flesh. At the same moment, human consciousness is swept away and the mind is flooded by atavistic visions and impulses. At this point, you may let the experience flow freely, exploring the powers of the demon, or you may focus the energies upon a specific target. In works of self-empowerment, Kusarikku fortifies the aura, transforming it into protective armor of golden crystalline light. In rites of malediction, his essence can be used to burn the soul of the victim and to weaken the body through diseases that deprive it of natural moisture and cause the flesh to wither, such as e.g. respiratory disorders. Envision yourself in the shape of the demon, channeling his powers from within, and breathe the burning force into the target's mouth, visualizing how it gathers in the lungs, exploding and spreading through the veins over the whole body. When you wish to finish the working, return to your mundane consciousness, thank the demon and close the ritual.

MEDITATION: THE THRONE IN THE DESERT

Envision yourself standing in the desert. The sun is high in the sky, shedding golden rays over the whole landscape. Start chanting the name of the demon and see how he rises and forms from the desert sands. He has the head and the lower part of the body shaped like a bull, but human torso and arms. He is sitting on a gigantic throne carved in crystallized sand. When he blows a pinch of sand into the air, violent sandstorms arise. When he stomps, the earth quakes and civilizations crumble to dust. When he walks through the desert, he molds golems from the sand and animates them. This is his army with which he rules the desert. Suddenly, he looks straight into your eyes, reaches down and lifts you up. He is so huge that you easily fit on the palm of his hand. He breathes his essence into your third eye and you switch places. Your consciousness expands and you are now the giant lord of the desert, while the creature which rests in your hand is only a small vessel of clay. The powers of the demon are now yours to command. Experiment with them, use them for creation or destruction. See how you can give the shape to your dreams and fantasies, or let the vision flow freely and simply enjoy the communion with the Lord of the Desert.

DREAM WORK: DIAMOND PORTAL

Before going to sleep, focus on the sigil of Kusarikku and keep chanting the name of the demon until you can sense his presence. At the same time, envision his golden energy pouring into the room through the sigil. When the atmosphere is slightly charged, trace the Key of the Night in front of you and speak the words of dream invocation:

> In the name of Tiamat,
> I stir the Black Waters of the Abyss,
> And I lift the Veil of the Night
> To gaze into mysteries which lie beyond the world of Waking.
> In the name of the Mother,
> I call Kusarikku to be my guide and companion through dreams and nightmares.
> By the Key of the Night I open the Gateways to Dreamlands,

And I seek to rest in the Arms of the Dragon,
In a dream which will take me to the Golden Desert,
Where I shall meet the Ancient Bull Demon,
And learn how to summon the winds to rise.
So it shall be!

Place the sigil below the pillow and when you lie down on the bed, close your eyes and envision a door with the symbol of the spirit. The symbol glows with warm golden light and the door opens for you to walk through. Focus on visualization given below and, while falling asleep, keep your mind focused on the intent of continuing the vision in a dream.

As you walk through the door of sleep, visualize yourself floating quietly in the black Void. Nothing exists here and the only thing you can see is a swirling black diamond. It sheds rays of purple light which function as a portal and you can feel that you are being drawn into the vortex of this strange energy. For a moment, you can only see a swirling cross with four equal arms that resemble tentacles moving counter-clockwise in fast rotation. Suddenly, a completely new scene begins to crystallize before your eyes. You are in the desert, the sun shines above and the sand looks like made of golden dust. In the distance, you see hundreds of pyramids. This looks like a city made of sand but with pyramids instead of buildings. Call the name of the demon. You will see how he arises from the sand and assumes the shape of a gigantic bull or bull-man. Ask him to guide you through the dreams and focus on this vision while falling asleep.

DRACONIAN SIGIL OF KUSARIKKU

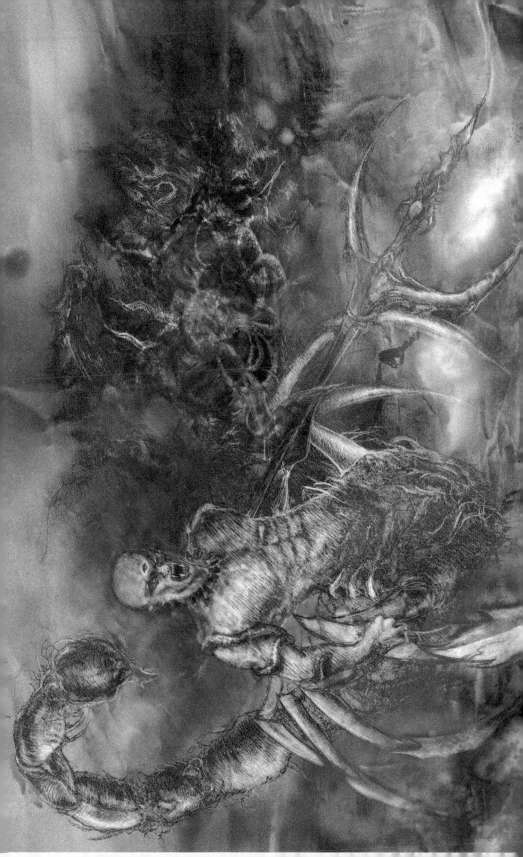

KINGU

In the *Enuma Elish*, Kingu, or Qingu, was the second husband of Tiamat, her son, consort, and commander of the forces of Chaos. She elevated him as the ruler over all the gods by giving him the Tablets of Destiny, the emblem of the supreme authority over the whole universe. When Tiamat was slain by Marduk, Kingu was imprisoned along with the other deities who had sided with the Mother Goddess. Eventually, he was sacrificed and his blood was mixed with earth in order to mould the first human beings. As one of the dead gods, he is now supposed to dwell in the Underworld, in the kingdom of shadows. His blood, however, lives in each human being as the legacy of the Forgotten Gods.

The Tablets of Destiny, or the Tablet of Destinies, was reputedly a clay tablet inscribed with cuneiform writing, a legal document, on which all decisions of the gods were recorded. Whoever held the tablets, ruled the universe. Sometimes they were identified with the concept of the *Me*, the divine decrees, the powers underlying the foundation of all civilization: social institutions, religious practices, technologies, morals and all kinds of human behaviour and conditions. According to legends and stories, there were either three tablets or one, which Kingu wore as a breastplate in the battle against the army of Marduk. Within the rites of magic, however, the Demon God often appears with twelve tablets, worn around the neck in the shape of a necklace. They are made of dark, unearthly substance, and they look like memory bars with information about the whole universe and all creation recorded in their layers. They represent the knowledge that was lost with the fall of the Primordial Gods and is occasionally tapped and recovered by humanity in the pursuit of technology and science. In metaphorical sense, the recovery of this knowledge bestows the authority over the universe and grants the power to influence the lives and the fates of all living beings, the power over life and death. Hence, the stories about gods fighting over the tablets, monsters and demons trying to steal them for their own purpose, and the legends of mythical powers attributed to those who ever held the Destinies.

In rites of evocation, Kingu appears as a demon-warrior, with snake skin and fiery eyes. He is red and his energy is red as well, manifesting as tongues of crimson flame. Snakes coil around his arms and he holds a fiery trident in his hand. He is furious, fierce and virile. He rarely communicates by verbal means and he will rather pierce your third eye with his flaming gaze and speak to you from within than converse in any traditional way.

Kingu also comes in his scorpion form, as half-man half-scorpion, red and fiery. He has human torso and head, the tail of a scorpion, but his human parts are covered with scales, like the body of a dragon or a serpent. His eyes are burning with red flames and fiery snakes coil around his arms. He inspires visions of underground temples lit by red or purple light, where blood is poured over sacrificial altars, and where the army of demons gathers at his command. In works of invocation, when his powers are bestowed on the practitioner, he grants the authority and leadership over the hordes of fiends and monsters lying in wait behind the Gates of the Night. This is the power to command legions of familiars, forces of Primordial Chaos, which can be used in rites of malediction or bound as guardians of the Temple. If you wish to bind them as familiar spirits, though, you also have to feed them on a regular basis with blood offerings, as these are blood-thirsty entities, ever hungry for the life-force of man, the essence of the Dragon.

The ritual provided below invokes the essence of Kingu to manifest from within. When invoked, he comes as a swirling vortex of fire, consuming the practitioner within and without. The boundaries of flesh are dissolved and the soul rises on tongues of flame, empowered by the fierce energy of the Demon God. This energy is dynamic and aggressive, ecstatic and overwhelming, sexual, burning, and penetrating. It can be used for rites of destruction or to fortify the subtle body of the practitioner through the works of spiritual alchemy. It also grants the authority over the other eleven demons of Tiamat, and it might be recommended to use the possession rite of Kingu before embarking on the further work with these entities.

INVOCATION OF KINGU

Light a few red candles and prepare the ritual blade. Burn strong incense, Musk or Dragon's Blood. Place the sigil of Kingu on the altar, make an offering of your own blood and trace the lines of the sigil, visualizing how it comes alive, activated by your life-essence. Envision it shining and burning with red flames, transforming the piece of parchment into a living gateway. This being done, place a drop of blood on your third eye as well.

Concentrate for a while on the sigil, sending the intent of the ritual through the Gate, and when you feel ready to being the invocation, draw the Key of the Night with the ritual blade, in front of you, and speak the words:

Kingu, Ruler of the Void,
First among the Gods of Fury,
Your blood flows through the veins of every human being,
You hold the Tablets of Destiny
The Keys to the Gates of the Dragon,
Where Liers-In-Wait guard the Lost Knowledge,
Awaiting the return of Primordial Gods,
When the world will reawaken through the power contained in
human blood,
The ancient legacy of the Dragon.
Kingu, fierce scorpion god,
Guardian of forgotten wisdom,
Come forth from the Womb of the Dragon!
Awaken from the arms of She who holds the world in her timeless
embrace!

Arise through blood which I offer you in this ritual,
Manifest through the life substance which I spill in your name!

Kingu welcomes and enjoys blood being spilt in the Temple. If you choose to empower the ritual by making an offering of a living being, this should be done at this point. If you work with your own blood only, focus now again on the sigil, envisioning the red flames rising up and spreading onto the whole ritual space, tongues of fire consuming everything around, dancing, flickering, and gliding over your skin.

Father of mankind,
Give me the Tablets of Destiny,
And grant me the power to use them,
So that I could rise proud and powerful,
Fortified by the primal essence of the Dragon!
Reveal to me the gnosis of blood that is hidden from the eyes of the profane,
Give me the power to command your army of demons,
To summon those who carry the force of the Void!
Awaken your fire and fury within me,
Overcome my weakness with persistence!
Enter my flesh and inflame my soul with your Draconian force,
So that I could carry the torch of victory
Over the mindless ignorance of the weak,
Treading upon corpses of those
Who choose slavery instead of lust and power!
Lord of Flames,
Awaken my body, my soul, my blood,
Inflame the spark of Divinity within,
Enter my Temple,
And join me in the sacred and unholy sacrament of spirit and flesh!
Come with tongues of fire dancing around,
Consuming the illusions of the world,
And awaken humanity from the slumber of oblivion!
Arouse the hunger for knowledge,
And let mankind rise and reach out for their Destinies!

Envision the flames entering your flesh, rising up from within and consuming your body in burning ecstasy. Feel how the atmosphere in the

Temple changes and becomes dense, filled with hot, fiery air. The flames are all around and you are the living flame, as well.

Father of those who walk upon the earth,
Upon the body of the Dragon,
Rise up with your flames and emblaze me from within!
Let your force flow through my body in my seething blood!
I seek your power, your essence, your source of being!
I create you and I summon you to arise,
For I am the Dragon,
I am the Beginning and the End of all things,
The all-seeing Eye and the ever-gaping Womb.
And I summon you in the name of She who created you,
In the name of Tiamat, the Mother and the Consort.
In the name of the Dragon,
Ho Ophis Ho Archaios,
Ho Drakon Ho Megas!

Burn the parchment with the sigil and let the invocation arise through the Gates of the Night. Envision Kingu, the fiery demon-warrior, entering the Temple and facing you, piercing your flesh and your soul with his fearsome gaze. When you are ready to merge with his essence, speak the final words of the invocation.

I am the wanderer on the Path of the Dragon,
I descend into the Heart of Darkness and ascend to the Heights of
Heaven,
I die and arise reborn,
I devour and become stronger,
I create my own Destiny,
I create my Path,
I create myself.
I am the spark of fire that is born in the Womb of the Dragon
And the raging blaze that will consume the world at the end of the
cycle.
I am the commander of the army of monsters,
Demons from a time beyond Time,
I travel among the stars and I gaze into the faces of gods,
With my blood I open the Gate to the Outside,

And I summon the hordes of fiends to do my bidding!
I am first among the Gods of Prey,
I am Kingu!

Visualize how the God enters your flesh and your soul, spreading over your whole being as liquid fire, stirring the blood in intoxicating ecstasy of senses. Feel the mystical union when your consciousness merges with the fiery essence of Kingu. Let the vision flow freely until the communion is finished. You can also use the visualization provided below and enter the trance of possession through meditation.

MEDITATION

Sit of lie down in a comfortable position. Envision yourself in mountainous area, standing on a rocky cliff, facing the setting sun. You look down below, where monsters, demons and fiends gather together. There are legions of them. Angry, furious, and hungry, awaiting their commander to arrive and lead them to battle. The sun descends to the horizon and turns red, painting the sky with blood-red colors. Shadows begin to appear and the whole atmosphere gets ominous, electrified. You can feel their anxiety and you see the burning hunger in their eyes.

Suddenly, the fiery Warrior-God manifests in front of you. His skin is red and covered by scales, like the body of a snake or a dragon. He is holding a burning trident in his right hand. Snakes coil around his arms. He faces you and gives you the trident. Then, he puts his hands on your shoulders and pierces you with his flaming gaze. His eyes burn with fire and you can feel this fiery energy entering your whole being, consuming you from within in blazing agony. Instead of the Demon-God, you can now see the swirling vortex of fire that absorbs you, or perhaps you absorb the fire. You can no longer tell the difference as your consciousness merges with the fiery essence of Kingu in ecstatic communion.

Let the vision flow freely for a while. When the transformation is complete, envision yourself in the form of the fiery Warrior-God, holding the burning trident in your right hand. Look around. All eyes are now fixed on you. You are Kingu. The hordes of the Void are now yours to command.

This trance of possession and the assumption of the godform of Kingu can be used in the further work with any of the eleven demon-gods described in this book. If done properly, it grants you the power to command the legions of fiends and monsters lurking behind the Gates of the Night, to awaken and summon them to do your bidding. Kingu is the ruler of these entities and the mediator between the forces of Chaos which exist outside the Gates and the human practitioner who seeks to access this timeless cosmic Current and to channel their power into the works of magic.

BOOK 3

APPENDICES

APPENDIX 1
ALCHEMICAL REBIRTH IN THE WATERS OF TIAMAT

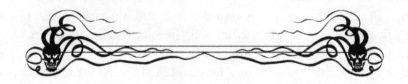

it in a comfortable position. Close your eyes. Breathe deeply in a steady rhythm. With each breath, start to relax and, as you enter the trance, begin the visualization:

Envision yourself standing on the shore of a black sea at night. The sea is calm and you can sense the watery breeze on your face. There are clouds in the sky covering the moon, but the stars are visible.

Disrobe and enter the water. Slowly start walking deeper and deeper into the sea. Immerse yourself in the water so that it covers you completely. Envision black watery serpents swimming around you and gliding over your skin. Start breathing under the water and feel how your body is being infused with the salt contained in the sea. Feel how the salt enters through your skin and through breathing into your lungs. Feel how it spreads over your whole body. This feels painful at first, but at the same time, you experience the pleasure of being united with the Primordial Darkness. Feel how your flesh is being dissolved in the watery womb of the Goddess Tiamat. The waters around you become black and all you can see is darkness. You are dissolving in this darkness, your body slowly becomes the black liquid which merges with the black water that surrounds you. You feel how your consciousness merges with the universe, before your eyes appear images and visions of all aspects of human life and death. At the same time, you are transforming and you undergo purification. All that was weak and imperfect in you is now dissolved in the waters, and what remains is your core, immortal essence, the spark of Divinity.

Visualize now that you are swimming up to the surface of the sea and then, floating on the waters, as if you were lying on your back and looking at the sky above you. The clouds move away and the full face of the moon appears in the sky. You feel purified and very light, bathing in the silver energy of the moon. The sky becomes brighter and brighter, and it is dawning. The moon disappears and the sun rises at the horizon. A new day begins.

Feel now how your divine spark rises from within and turns into a flame. The flame within you is getting bigger and warmer, increasing with the passage of the sun over the horizon. The sun warms the waters of the sea and you feel how the enormous heat spreads from the base of your spine and consumes your whole body in tongues of red fire. As the sun reaches its peak at noon, you are the living flame, the essence of fire, floating up above the waters – once black, now clear and shining with the golden reflection of the sun. The feeling is ecstatic and you burn with delight and sensation of total power.

As the sun sets down and slowly descends towards the horizon, you feel how the fire within you becomes crystallized into flesh. Your former body that was dissolved in the black waters is gone, and a new one is being created. Feel and see how it is being built and how the fire is transformed into flesh. You are now again in your physical body, but the flame and the feeling of power within you still remain and bind your spirit and your flesh together.

When the sun disappears behind the horizon and the night starts again, you swim towards the shore and emerge out of the sea–strengthened and rejuvenated: reborn in the dark waters of Tiamat. Your alchemical transformation is complete and you feel the unity of forces within your body and your soul. You are a unified consciousness, an isolated and unique being in the whole universe, yet connected with the cosmic awareness. Meditate upon this feeling for a while, then return to your Temple.

COMMENTARY:

The meditation reflects the four main alchemical processes of spiritual transformation. Immersion in the waters of Tiamat represents the first, initiatory process: the alchemical *solutio* or the *Nigredo* (Blackening). Water is the principle of dissolution which disintegrates and purifies the imperfect body of the initiate. This is the essence of primordial chaos and entropy, represented in mythologies as the Dragon Goddess Tiamat. In alchemy, the salt that causes putrefaction is called "the spume of Typhon," which refers to another sea monster related to Tiamat. The Pythagoreans called the oceanic waters "the Tear of Kronos" because of their salty quality. The body immersed in the sea also dissolves into black salt which is then purified into the white essence of wisdom.

The waters of Tiamat are the primordial womb which contains all potentialities: all four elements and all potential life. It is the matrix of all creation. In psychological sense, they represent the collective unconscious. Purification and distillation of the flesh and the spirit in the black waters of Tiamat bring the practitioner to the focus on transcendent consciousness and the principle of alchemical coagulation – self re-creation.

This process of re-creation begins at the next stage of alchemical *Magnum Opus* – the *Albedo* (Whitening) in which the prime matter is purified. The next step is taken at the stage of the *Citrinitas* (Yellowing), which ennobles the prime matter. The final transmutation is accomplished at the stage of the *Rubedo* (Reddening), which also represents the ascent of the Kundalini. This is symbolized by the sun entering the zenith. The consciousness is unified and the process of re-creation or coagulation is complete. The flesh and the spirit are rejuvenated and the practitioner emerges out of the waters, like a new-born child leaves the maternal womb.

The Ritual of Tiamat and Kingu

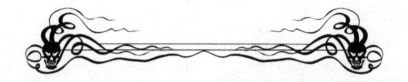

The ritual is designed for two practitioners, one invoking the black, dissolving essence of Tiamat, the other assuming the red, fiery godform of Kingu. Ideally, the ceremony should be performed by a female and a male practitioner, providing suitable vessels for the energies. Depending on participants' choice, the sacrament of communion may be consumed purely on spiritual level or through sexual union, transforming the feast of flesh into ecstasy of the spirit.

The purpose of the ritual is to awaken the power of Kingu, the Dragon Within, by activating the demonic element that is contained in human blood, and to unite it with the energy of Tiamat, the Dragon Without. Therefore, a sacrifice of blood is necessary, and an offering of sexual fluids is recommended. Solitary practitioners can perform this working without a partner. This can be done in two ways: either by invoking the energy of one godform into the temple of flesh and evoking the other to physical manifestation, or by invoking both deities in order to experience the communion of the energies from within. It can also be performed as a group ritual, with the Magus and the Priestess leading the ceremony and channeling the energies upon the other participants.

The text of the ritual includes quotations from the *Enuma Elish*[13]. You will need a ritual blade, a chalice filled with red wine, representing the blood of the Dragon, and enough candles to light up the Temple. Black and red candles are specifically recommended for the working.

---

[13]   Translation by L.W. King

The Magus and the Priestess together:

In Nomine Draconis!
Ho Ophis Ho Archaios,
Ho Drakon Ho Megas!

The Priestess:

Ummu-Hubur who formed all things,
spawned monster-serpents,
Sharp of tooth and merciless of fang;
With poison, instead of blood, she filled their bodies.
Fierce monster-vipers she clothed with terror,
With splendor she decked them, she made them of lofty stature.
Whoever beheld them, terror overcame him,
And none could withstand their attack.
They bore cruel weapons, without fear of the fight.
Her commands were mighty, none could resist them;
Among the gods who were her sons, she exalted Kingu;
In their midst she raised him to power.
To march before the forces, to lead the host,
To give the battle-signal, to advance to the attack,
To direct the battle, to control the fight,
She gave him the Tablets of Destiny, on his breast she laid them.
And she cried out: "Let us wage war!"

The Magus

I invoke Kingu, commander of the hordes of the Void,
The Lord of Destiny and the ruler of this world!
I summon the one whose immortal essence flows through our veins,
Whose power has never been defeated, for it exists in human blood!
Kingu! Rise up with fire and fury!
Come through the Gate of Darkness!
Arise from unquiet waters of Primal Chaos,
Awaken the blood and stir the ocean of dreams!
And enter this Temple,
Through the feast of flesh and blood!
I offer my body to be consumed, dissolved, reborn, awakened, and

empowered!
You are the Key to the Abyss of the Void,
Your blood opens the gateways to the Kingdom of the Night,
You are the Guardian of the Threshold,
The power Within and Without,
First among the Gods of Fury,
Lord of those who wake up and rise in the name of the Dragon,
Transformed and forged in Draconian Fire,
Walk with me!
Let your flames illuminate my Path,
Let your force guide me through the Darkness of the Void,
On my quest for Gnosis,
Give me the Tablets of Destiny
And reveal to me the Way to Divinity!
Come to me, Kingu!
I call you in the name of the Mother,
In the name of Tiamat!

The Magus and the Priestess together:

In Nomine Draconis!
Ho Ophis Ho Archaios,
Ho Drakon Ho Megas!

The practitioners visualize the army of demons, Children of Tiamat, led by Kingu – the human-like god-demon; on his chest hang the Tablets of Destiny.

The Priestess:

I invoke Tiamat, Mother of Gods,
Primal Dragon Goddess,
Queen of the Kingdom of the Night!
I summon the one who is before all things,
Whose body is the flesh of the earth,
Ancient Serpent who holds the world in her timeless coils!
Come to me, Tiamat!
Your breath is the raging hurricane,
Your heat is the rampant flame that wreaks havoc across the land,

You are the flooding waters and the fearsome tempests,
The consuming and the nourishing force of the world!
I seek your Power and Knowledge,
Your Darkness, your Blood, your Primal Essence!
Rise up from your resting place beneath the Mountains of the West,
Where the sun descends at night and the moon rests by day.
Come through the Gates of the Night,
Enter my flesh and inflame my soul,
Through the primal ecstasy of senses,
In agony of torture and delight!
I offer my body to be consumed, awakened and fortified by your
Draconian Essence!
I descend into the black waters of the Void,
Into the Womb of Chaos,
And I arise reborn as the Ancient Dragon Goddess,
The living incarnation of the Divine!
I am the Mother of All Things,
The Beginning and the End,
I am the Dragon,
I am Tiamat!

The Magus and the Priestess together:

IA HUBUR!
IA MUMMU!
IA TEHOM!
IA TIAMAT!

The practitioners envision the Dragon Goddess of Chaos, Tiamat, as she rises from the Void and joins the army of demons led by Kingu.

The Priestess draws the seal of Kingu with her blood on the body of the Magus, saying:

I utter your spell, in the assembly of the gods I raise you to power,
The dominion over all the gods is yours,
Be thou exalted, my chosen spouse.

The Magus draws the seal of Tiamat with his blood on the body of the Priestess, saying:

Let the opening of your mouth quench the Fire-god;
Who is exalted in the battle, let him display his might!

The Priestess raises the chalice and speaks:

We drink the Blood of the Dragon and offer our
own in return, the living essence of Kingu.

They both drink the wine that represents the Blood of the Dragon, and make a sacrifice of their own blood. If the ritual is conducted outdoors, the blood should be poured onto the ritual blade which is then thrust into the ground. If the participants perform the working in the Temple, the blood should be poured into the chalice and drunk with the wine.

The Priestess:

May Tiamat and Kingu unite in the unholy sacrament of flesh
and soul! May our blood unite with the Body of the Dragon, the
immortal Essence of Tiamat, as we offer ourselves to be consumed
by primordial Darkness and Fire! We invoke the power of
Kingu, the essence of Forgotten Gods, to awaken in our veins!

For man is of the Blood of Darkness but has the Spirit of
Light breathed into his flesh. And the body of man belongs
to the Primal Gods, and the blood of man is the Blood of the
Dragon, but his mind is turned towards the Gods of Light.
And this is the War which shall be always fought until the
Dragon re-awakens and rises up to the stars. Then the Primal
Waters will meet again and the World will be One.

The Magus:

And so it is done!

Envision the battle in which Kingu and Tiamat and their army of demons face the forces of Light. Watch as the Goddess is slain and from her body, the earth is created, and from the earth, the human being. Visualize how man awakens to life by the power of Kingu's blood. Feel the relationship between these two primordial principles. Your flesh is a part of Tiamat. Your blood is a part of Kingu. Feel how the essence of the Primal Gods awakens in your body and in your soul through blood and fire. Merge your consciousness with the primordial darkness that is a part of you and from which you were born to life. Let the vision flow freely and enjoy the communion of the forces.

SEAL OF TIAMAT

SEAL OF KINGU

MALEDICTION OF BLOOD

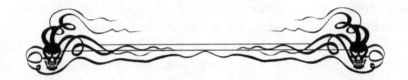

CURSING RITUAL

repare a puppet that will be used in the ritual as a vessel for the soul of the target. It is recommended to sew it from black cloth and it has to be small enough to fit into your hand. Stuff the puppet with any suitable material, including ingredients which symbolize the four elements: incense for air, soil for earth, sulphur for fire and oil for water. You may also include other symbols of life, such as e.g. grain and ingredients connected with death, such as graveyard dust. Write the name of the victim with blood on a piece of parchment and put it in the place of the heart. If you have sympathetic links to your target, such as hair, blood, nails, etc. put them into the puppet, as well, but these are not essential for the ritual. Finally, stick the photo or an image of the victim's face onto the head of the puppet. Prepare pins and red cord with which you will stab and bind the victim's soul through the planes. You will also need a piece of black cloth to wrap the puppet and a handful of graveyard soil. When all preparations are complete, you may start the ritual. It is best to perform the cursing work at late hours of the night, when your victim is asleep and will not be able to resist the attack or strike back. Perform the ritual in a black robe with a hood covering your face.

BAPTISM OF BLOOD

Place the puppet in the Qlipothic Star, with the Seal of Tiamat on the left and the Seal of Kingu on the right. Burn Dragon's Blood incense and light black candles. Trace the Key of the Night in the air above the altar and envision it shining with Draconian flames, empowering the Temple and opening hidden gateways between worlds and dimensions. Envision the Temple in the heart of the Void, far from mundane world, where nothing exists except your Will and your consciousness. This is the Womb of the Night where souls are born and destroyed. Your mind is a part of this timeless force. Nothing can withstand your power, and the whole universe must bend to your Will.

Anoint the puppet with your blood and breathe the spark of life to make it a living being. You can also use sexual fluids to bring the puppet to life and empower the manifestation of Draconian energies. When this is done, hold the puppet in your projecting hand and recite the words:

In the name of the Mother
Who is the Beginning and the End of all that exists,
By the power of the four elements
Which compose the flesh of all living beings,
And by the timeless force of life contained in my blood,
The Essence of the Dragon,
I summon you to live and feel,
Awaken and rise at my command!
I, (your magical name), baptize you with the name NN
Your body is the body of NN,
Your mind is the mind of NN.
And I bind the soul of NN to this vessel.
You, NN, and this puppet are now as one:
What it feels, you will feel,
When it hurts, you will hurt,
And when it dies and crumbles to dust, you will die too,
Your cursed soul will leave the mortal flesh,
And will be devoured by the monsters of the Void.
In the name of Tiamat who delivers and devours worlds and souls,
And by the power of Kingu who is the father of the human race,
I summon you, NN, into this mortal vessel!
Your body and soul are now mine to do as I please!

Feel how the soul of the target is being drawn into the vessel and envision that you are holding the real person, helpless and unable to escape.

When the baptism is finished, and the soul is bound to the puppet, summon the Eleven Monsters of the Void to deliver the Curse.

EVOCATION

By the Blood of the Dragon,
And in the name of Tiamat,
I open the Gates of the Night,
And I call the Eleven Demons of the Void
To come and assist me in my Work!
In the name of Kingu,
I summon you to manifest in this Temple!
Awaken from your slumber in the Womb of Primal Chaos,
Rise through the Gates of the Dragon,
And deliver death, sickness and misery upon my enemy,
Feast on his flesh and devour his soul,
Consume his vital essence from within
And leave his mortal body to wither and die in agonizing pain!
Let maggots feed on his rotting corpse,
And burn his tortured soul so that he could never be reborn again!
I, (your magical name), curse (the name of the victim), in the name
of the Dragon!
By the power of Kingu and the Mighty Eleven,
In Nomine Tiamat
Ho Ophis Ho Archaios
Ho Drakon Ho Megas!

Children of Tiamat, I call you to come forth
and deliver death to my enemy!

Mušmahhu, Blind Serpent of Primordial Void,
Arise from forgotten forests and dark caves in the bowels of the
earth,
Spit the venom upon the eyes of NN so he may not see me,
Paralyze his tongue so he may not reverse the spell,
And fill his ears with your fearsome hissing to make him tremble in

fear,
Deaf, blind, mute, and helpless!

(stab the puppet in the eyes, in the ears and in the mouth)

Ušumgallu, Fearsome Cobra with scales of gold,
Fearless killer and destroyer of the weak,
Arise from forgotten worlds beyond the stars, from subterranean
labyrinths and underwater temples,
Coil around the flesh and the soul of NN,
Trap his soul in this mortal vessel,
And hold him firm in your deadly embrace so
that he may not escape the torture!

(stab the puppet in the top of the head)

Ugallu, Mighty Storm Demon who comes with roaring hurricanes,
Arise from unquiet waters in the Womb of Chaos,
Rip the aura of NN and shatter his shields and defenses!
Scorch his flesh with your whips of lightning
and tear his tortured soul to pieces!

(stab the puppet in the third eye)

Girtablullû, Mighty Scorpion who comes with
burning rays of the rising sun,
Arise from deserted cities beneath the blood-dyed desert,
And turn the blood of NN into burning poison,
Paralyze his limbs so that he could not strike back,
And take away his strength, confidence and will to fight.

(stab the arms and legs of the puppet and tie them with the red cord)

Lahamu, Demon Warrior who comes with fire and fury,
Arise from blood-dyed battlefields behind the Gate of Sunset,
And pierce the soul of NN with your flaming lashes,

Torture his wretched body with your lighting force,
And leave him writhing and screaming in agony!

(stab the puppet in the throat)

Mušuššu, Furious Wraith who feeds on the hearts of the weak,
Arise from the kingdom of Shadows with
serpents and phantoms of the Night
Mesmerize NN with your hypnotic stare and
poison his dreams with horror and nightmares
So that he may not find a peaceful rest.
Drain his vital essence until there is nothing
left, rip his chest and devour his heart!

(stab the puppet in the heart)

Ūmu Dabrūtu, Fearsome Demon of Blazing Tempests,
Arise from the Vortex of Chaos, with furious storms and raging
winds,
Strike NN with bolts of lightning and burning lashes!
Tear down his world, take away his happiness and prosperity,
destroy his family and relationships,
And fill his life with terror and gloom!

(stab the puppet in the solar plexus)

Kulullû, Flesh Eating Demon of decay and putrefaction,
Arise from cold temples beneath dead seas and black oceans,
Intoxicate the soul of NN with your festering essence and turn his
dreams into unspeakable nightmares,
Feast on his vital juices and deprive him of virility,
Fill his body with your venom and stench
and make him rot from within!

(stab the puppet in the genitals)

Bašmu, Venomous Serpent who swallows the sun
and destroys worlds in apocalyptic fire,
Arise from black waters in the land of no return,
Poison the blood of NN with your venomous flames,
Fill his lungs with suffocating smoke,
And consume his soul in burning agony!

(hold the puppet in thick clouds of smoke)

Kusarikku, Fearsome Bull who rules the Sands of Time,
Arise from forlorn deserts and barren wastelands,
Summon your harsh winds and take away the vital force of NN,
Burn his cursed soul and let his mortal body crumble to dust
So that it could be buried and forgotten by the living!

(throw graveyard soil on the puppet)

Uridimmu, Fierce Wolf Demon who comes with the roaring of lions,
Arise from the Black Desert in the heart of the Void,
Wrap the body and the soul of NN in your tremendous gloom,
Shatter his senses with your black wind and
take away the light from his life,
Leaving him lonely and despaired,
Forever lost in the wastelands of Everlasting Night!

(wrap the puppet with black cloth)

In the name of the Dragon,
This is my Will and so it is done!

Bury the puppet in the earth and recite the words:

Ashes to ashes,
Dust to dust.
As this vessel rots in the grave,
So you, NN, will rot from within.

And when the last spark of life leaves your mortal flesh,
Your death will be eternal.

Make a sacrifice of life, spilling the blood upon the burial place.
When this is done, finish the ritual with the words:

Kingu, fearsome Ruler of the Void,
I spill this blood in your name
Onto the body of the Dragon.
Accept my offering and let my Will be done.
In Nomine Draconis,
Ho Ophis Ho Archaios
Ho Drakon Ho Megas!

APPENDIX 4
THE UNDERWORLD

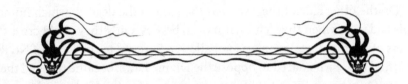

n Mesopotamian beliefs, the Netherworld was located either in the waters of Apsū or below, in the boundless Darkness that existed outside the structures of the world. While Apsū personified the underground ocean and the source of all fresh waters on the earth, the whole universe was surrounded by the primordial waters of Tiamat, the ocean of Primal Chaos, the Land of No Return. The Netherworld represented the cosmic concept of the empty space between the earth's crust and the primeval sea. There are many stories and legends about the Underworld, and the origins of the myth vary depending on the historical period. Generally, it was believed that either the waters of Apsū were the land of death itself or this realm was located somewhere nearby. It was separated from the world of the living by an underground river Hubur (or *id lu rugu*, which in Sumerian meant "the river which block's a man's way"), and the crossing of the river was equivalent with the final separation from the world of man after which the soul came to dwell in the realm of shadows for eternity.

The concept of the journey across the River of the Underworld is encountered in many cultures, e.g. also in ancient Greece or Egypt. Usually, a discarnate soul travelled to the realm of the dead in assistance of a ghastly ferryman. It was so in Greek mythology, where dead people had to cross Styx in Charon's boat, the legend which is probably familiar to most of the readers. But, the roots of the story are found in the Sumerian lore. In the famous epic of Gilgamesh, the hero crosses the waters of death with the help of Ur-shanabi, a demonic ferryman. Not much is known about him from the myth itself, but in the story he is associated with *umu*-snakes, the primordial monsters of Tiamat, therefore we might assume that he is one of the demonic beings created by the Dragon Goddess, who gained a new function in the Divine Order. There is also a neo-Assyrian poem of the vision of the Underworld in which we encounter another demonic ferryman named Humut-tabal, which means "hurry and take away," described in the story as a horrible monster.

On the other side of the river was the land of the dead to which human souls had to go when they left their mortal bodies. Only they could cross the waters of death. Mortal man was not allowed to travel to the Land of No Return, and those who dared to oppose the Divine Laws, became trapped there forever. Only heroes such as Gilgamesh, who went to the Underworld to visit his dead friend Enkidu, could embark on such a journey and return alive. Also, there are stories of gods descending to the realm of shadows, such as the popular myth of the goddess Inanna, who descended from the heavens to the Underworld, was torn apart by the demons, reborn, and returned victoriously to the world of Light.

Descriptions of the realm of death depict a rather somber and dire vision of the afterlife, roughly corresponding to the *sheol* of the ancient Hebrews. The Mesopotamian Underworld was the land devoid of any light, full of dust, and there was no water to drink. It was called "the home which one may enter, but never leave," "the road from which there is no return" and "the dwelling where those entering find blindness."[14] The spirits of the dead were either naked or with wings of birds. Souls wandered hopelessly in search for food, but they did not find anything that could satiate their hunger. Those who were not forgotten by their relatives received food and drinks in the form of offerings left at the graves. But, the souls whose families were no longer among the living had to suffer the fate of endless wandering through the underground kingdom in great tortures and agony. The worst suffering, however, was left for those whose corpses were not buried properly. They became phantoms and haunted the Underworld, and sometimes they also visited the world of man in search for oblivion or in order to torture the living. It is also significant that in the realm of death all souls were equal. From the epic of Gilgamesh, we learn that even kings and emperors suffered the same fate as the souls of servants and slaves. There were also spirits who became demons. The Underworld was the abode of the *gidim* (Akkadian *etemmu*), restless souls who had to be propitiated by offerings of food, drink, and olive (the offering was called *kispu*). This was the duty of the dead per-

---

[14] Francois Lenormant: *Chaldean Magic. Its Origin and Development*

son's family and relatives. It was believed that the *gidim,* when deprived of food, might become vicious and return from the Underworld to haunt and torture the living. They could even possess a living person by entering the body through ears, or they caused painful and deadly diseases: e.g. there was a psychic disorder called *qāt et* (literally "the hand of the ghost"), or *sibit etemmi* ("seizure by a ghost"), which had physical symptoms of an illness but was believed to be a form of possession.

The Underworld was associated with many names and attributes: *arali, irkalla, kukku, ekur, kigal, ganzir,* or simplu *ki, kur* (Sumerian "earth"), or the Akkadian *ersetu.* The land of the dead was called "the land of no return," "the desert" or "the great below." It was usually located far away, in an unknown distance, often in the west or south-west. However, these depictions are different in each myth, epic and legend. Sumerian accounts locate the Underworld east of Mesopotamia. Its entrance was in the mountains and the gate was *ganzir,* to which the soul descended down the long stairway. At the gate, there was a guardian who watched to ensure that no one, apart from the dead souls, entered the land of death. In the myth of Inanna's descent into the Underworld we encounter a guardian named Neti. In other accounts, these are the twin brothers, Lugal-irra and Meslamta-ea, standing at the left and the right sides of the gate. In Mesopotamian artwork, each of them is depicted with an axe and a club. Sometimes, the entrance to the Netherworld was watched by the Scorpion Man, alone or assisted by other similar beings. However, there are also sources which do not mention any creatures guarding the gate at all.

The rulers of the Underworld were the goddess Ereshkigal and her husband Nergal. The name *Ereshkigal* is translated as the "Queen of the Great Below." She was also known as the Akkadian goddess Allatu. Her first husband was Gugal-ana. It was his funeral celebration that brought Inanna to the land of her dark sister, though there are several different versions of this myth as well. The son of Ereshkigal and Gugal-ana was Ninazu, the god whose sacred animal was the serpent-dragon (*mušhuššu*). After the death of her husband, the queen of the Underworld married Nergal, the violent and terrifying warrior-god. Nergal was believed to be the son of Enlil and Ninlil. He was also called Erra (but it was rather the name of another dark deity with whom Nergal was associated) and sometimes, he was identified with one of the twin brothers who guarded the gate, Meslamta-ea. The main centre of Nergal's worship was located in the Sumerian city of Kutha, the name of which became one of the names of the Underworld, specifically associated with the main city in the land of the dead. Originally, Nergal was the god of the sun heat, fever, and plague. He was responsible for fires and disasters. His planet was Mars. He was depicted in a long robe, with one leg stretched out, and with his foot on a dais or treading upon a human being. In his hand, he usually held a curved sword and a sceptre with lion heads. Together with Ereshkigal, he dwelt in the palace protected by seven gates. Each gate was locked and watched by a guardian. Everyone who wanted to pass through the gates had to leave all things connected with the world of the living, as it is presented in the myth of Inanna's descent into the Underworld. At the entrance of each gate, the guardian requested that she removed and left one article of clothing and jewelry. This is because the souls could enter the land of the dead only after breaking all ties with the world in which they lived before.

The souls travelling to the Underworld were not subjected to any judgment. Ereshkigal only sentenced them to death, and then their names were written on the tablets by the scribe, the goddess Geshtinana.[15] Other deities from Ereshkigal's retinue were: Ningishzida, Namtar, and Enmešarra. Ningishzida was the son of Ninazu. In Babylonian magical charms he appears as the keeper of the demons of the Underworld. His symbolic animal was the horned serpent or a dragon (bašmu), and in astrology, he was ascribed to the constellation of Hydra. Namtar was Ereshkigal's vizier and messenger. His name meant "destiny" or "fate." As we observed before, he was also a malevolent demon and a bringer of disease. Also, there was a group of deities called *Anunnaki* who were believed to reside in the land of the dead. They were the offspring of the sky god, Anu, and their number varied depending on a literary source, but generally, they were fifty creatures. Although originally they were deities of the earth and the sky, in the middle-Babylonian period, they came to be identified with the lower world, contrary to the deities of the sky, the *Igigi*. In certain accounts, the Anunnaki resided in the Underworld city of Irkalla, where they passed the judgment over the souls entering the Land of No Return.

Apart from discarnate souls of men, gods presiding over the land of death, and occasional visitors, we also encounter many demons and deities who reside in the Underworld after death. According to Mesopotamian

---

[15] There are sources which mention a sort of "judgment" of the dead but there are no details and the whole concept is very unclear.

beliefs, gods were not immortal, or in other words, not all gods possessed the gift of immortality. They did not die from natural causes, but were usually killed in fight. In Mesopotamian artwork, we often see gods fighting demons, monsters or deities and one slaying the other. Inanna, killed by Ereshkigal, is forced to stay in the Underworld until the gods of the heavens come to rescue her. The dead deities had to dwell in the Netherworld like the souls of humans. But, sometimes, the fate of the dead deities was unknown, as it is in the case of such "dead" gods as Tiamat, Apsū, Kingu or the demon, Humbaba (Huwawa), killed by Gilgamesh. The dead gods, however, were still worshipped and received offerings. It was believed that even though they dwell in the land of the dead, they still have their powers and can influence the world of the living. It was the same with the demons of Tiamat, even though slain by Marduk, they were still regarded as dangerous and deadly.

There were also legends in which the Sun God Shamash traveled at night to the Land of No Return as the Sun of the Underworld. It was believed that each day at sunset he descended to the land of death in order to shine the light over the lowest regions. This story resembles the Egyptian tale about the daily journey of the Sun God Ra into the Underworld realm of Amenti, from which he returned at sunrise. This journey was the cause why the lowest regions of the Underworld became associated with fire and heat which sometimes manifests on the earth in the form of volcanic eruptions. Nevertheless, in other accounts, Shamash rests at night not in the Underworld, but in the centre of heavens. A similar function is ascribed to god Nindara, who was the nocturnal sun, the sun of the Netherworld. Plunged in the regions of the night, he defeated the Darkness which surrounded him with his solar power and rose triumphant at the dawn of the day. He was a warrior god, an arbitrator, a judge, and a regulator of destiny[16]

Among Mesopotamian myths which describe the Underworld, one of the less known and the most interesting stories is the neo-Assyrian epic of the vision of the Other Side seen by the prince Kumaya. He prayed for a dream in which he could see when he was going to die. Having heard his prayers, the goddess, Ereshkigal, promised that she would show him what he wished to see. And so, in his following dream, he descended to the Underworld where he saw fifteen demonic creatures. They were so terrifying that he was unable to describe them. He also noticed a dark human figure

---

[16] Francois Lenormant: *Chaldean Magic. Its Origin and Development*

wearing a red cloak, and then he faced the angry god, Nergal. He was furious that the prince dared to enter the land of the dead and wanted to kill him, but the god, Ishum, came to protect him and the prince went back to the world of the living. It is often thought that this prince was Assurbanipal, the future king of the Assyrian Empire.

DESCENT INTO THE GREAT BELOW

The working is a visual journey to the Underworld, based on the imagery from myths and legends about the Mesopotamian land of death. It is designed as a path-working with the opening of the Gates and the invocation of the gods of the Underworld.

Place a few drops of your blood on a ritual blade and trace the Key of the Night in front of you. Envision how the Temple is being filled with Draconian energies and feel the Dragon's Fire rising from within, transforming and fortifying your spirit and your flesh.

When you feel ready to begin the ritual, open the Gates of the Night with the following invocation:

Ninghizhidda!
Serpent God of Irkalla,
Keeper of the Gates!
Open the entrance to the Great Below!
Open the door to the Underworld!
Open the passage to the land of the dead!
Open the door so that I may enter!
Or I will break down its bars,
I will attack the inclosure,
I will leap over its fences by force!
In the name of Tiamat,
And by the power of the Dragon,
Open the Gates of the Night,
Or I will cause the dead to rise and devour the living!
I will give the dead power over the living!
Guardian of the Underworld,
Grant me the way!
Let me into the Temple of the Dead!
Where souls dwell in darkness,

Where dust thickens upon the door,
Where shades wander in forgotten tombs!
Show me the sights hidden from the eyes of mortals,
And let me return to the world of the living,
Reborn and empowered by the Black Flame Within.
Ereshkigal, Queen of the Dead
Let me enter your dark kingdom!
Nergal, Lord of Darkness,
Open the door to the Land of No Return!
By the Blood of the Dragon
I open the Gates to the Heart of the Void!
In Nomine Draconis,
Ho Drakon Ho Megas!

Visualize yourself standing in a mountainous area, at the feet of the great Mountains of Mashu. You are facing the gate to the land of the dead. The entrance is guarded by two human figures, one of them is armed with an axe, the other with a club. Speak the words of greeting in the name of Tiamat, the Dragon of the Void, and ask them to open the gate for you. When this is done, walk through the door.

You are now on a long stairway which leads down, into the land of the dead. As you descend, it gets darker and darker, and after a while, all you can see is a strange red light. Now, you stand before the first gate to the Land of No Return. A demonic watcher comes to greet you and demands that you leave a piece of your clothing (or jewelry), which represents something personal, something that binds you to the mundane world. Whatever he asks, give it to the watcher, who will then let you walk through the gate, and continue your journey. The same happens at the remaining six gates. Each item you leave is meaningful and represents your attachment to the world of the living. You have to sacrifice it all before you can enter the land of the dead. There are seven gates to the Underworld and you have to pass this test at each of them. Take as much time as it is needed for this part of the journey. Meditate on what you are asked to leave behind and what these things mean to you. When you feel ready, proceed with the meditation.

You are now in the Underworld. It is full of dust and devoid of water. Souls wander endlessly in search for food which they cannot find. Those who suffer the worst agony are the souls of people who were not buried properly–these are the spectres who haunt the world of the dead and bring terror and gloom into the world of the living. Here, in the Underworld, all souls are equal. Apart from the souls of common people, you notice kings and dead deities. All of them are naked and some have wings like birds.

You are now approached by the *gidim,* the unquiet souls who bring misfortune upon the living. Give them food, drink and olive (it is also recommended to have these offerings on your altar during the ritual). They will guide you to the lower levels of the Underworld. Follow them into the Heart of Darkness. Ask them to show you the secrets of the Underworld. If you wish, they can also take you to the palace of the Queen Ereshkigal and her consort, the dark god Nergal. Let the vision flow freely and enjoy the experience. Let it empower you and fortify your Will and persistence on the Path. After you finish your trip, ask them to guide you back to the seven gates through which you entered. As you ascend through the gates, claim back what you have left or you may choose to leave it as a sacrifice to the Lords of the Underworld. This, however, should be a conscious and resolute decision.

Leave the land of the dead and ground yourself in your Temple. Meditate for a while on what you experienced and what the whole journey meant to you. Close the ritual and return to your mundane consciousness.

APPENDIX 5
BIBLIOGRAPHY

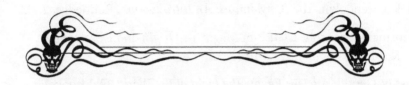

Black, Jeremy. Anthony Green. *Gods, Demons and Symbols of Ancient Mesopotamia: An Illustrated Dictionary*. University of Texas Press, 1992.

Campbell Thompson, R. *Devils and Evil Spirits of Babylonia*. Kessinger Publishing, 2010.

Dalley, Stephanie. *Myths from Mesopotamia: Creation, The Flood, Gilgamesh, and Others*. Oxford University Press, 2009.

Enuma Eliš czyli opowieść babilońska o powstaniu świata. Wydawnictwo Wacław Bagiński, 1998.

Jacobsen, Thorkild. *The Treasures of Darkness. A History of Mesopotamian Religion*. Yale University Press, 1976.

King, Leonard W. *Babylonian Magic and Sorcery*. Kessinger Publishing, 2003.

King, Leonard W. *Enuma Elish: The Seven Tablets of Creation, Vol 1 & 2*. Cosimo Classics, 2007.

Kramer, Samuel Noah. *History Begins at Sumer: Thirty-Nine Firsts in Recorder History*. University of Pennsylvania Press, 1981.

Kramer, Samuel Noah. The *Sumerians: Their History, Culture and Character*. University of Chicago Press, 1971.

Kramer, Samuel Noah. *Sumerian Mythology.* University of Pennsylvania Press, 1998.

Leick, Gwendolyn. *Sex & Eroticism in Mesopotamian Literature.* Routledge, 2003.

Leick, Gwendolyn. The *Babylonians: An Introduction.* Routledge, 2002.

Lenormant, Francois. *Chaldean Magic. Its Origin and Development.* Kessinger Publishing, 2010.

Massey, Gerald: *Ancient Egypt: The Light of the World.* Old Book Publishing, 2011.

Oates, Joan. *Babylon.* Thames & Hudson, 1986.

Pritchard, James B. Ancient *Near Eastern Texts Relating to the Old Testament.* Princeton University Press, 1969.

Smith, George. *Chaldean Account of Genesis.* Wizards Bookshelf, 1994.

Wallis Budge, E.A. *Amulets and Superstitions.* Kessinger Publishing, 2010.

Wiggerman, F.A.M. *Mesopotamian Protective Spirits: The Ritual Texts.* Brill Academic Pub, 1992.

CPSIA information can be obtained
at www.ICGtesting.com
Printed in the USA
BVHW082234140120
569366BV00003B/139/P